CHIYOGAMI

CHIYOGAMI

Hand-printed Patterned Papers of Japan

Ann Herring

KODANSHA INTERNATIONAL
Tokyo • New York • London

The author dedicates this book to her family—especially to Albert and Margaret Fromherz, and to her aunts, both here and in eternity: Mary Herring Hudson, Lucy Herring, Laura Saunders, Ella Herring, Bertha King, Lucy Fromherz, Esther King, Winifred Hill, Margaret King, Florence van Etten Bolinger, Dorothy Young, Geraldine King, Gladys King, and Louise King.

Photographs by Eiji Kōri and Tamiko Tanaka

Distributed in the United States by Kodansha America, Inc., 114 Fifth Avenue, New York, N.Y. 10011, and in the United Kingdom and continental Europe by Kodansha Europe Ltd., Gillingham House, 38-44 Gillingham Street, London SW1V 1HU. Published by Kodansha International Ltd., 17-14 Otowa 1-chome, Bunkyo-ku, Tokyo 112, and Kodansha America, Inc. Copyright © 1987, by Kodansha International Ltd. All rights reserved. Printed in Japan.
LCC 86-40438
ISBN 4-7700-1692-1
First edition, 1987
First paperback edition, 1992
  93 94 95 5 4 3 2

The title page shows chiyogami with a design of peonies on yellow ground. *Kobōsho-ban.* 1862. Author's collection.

CONTENTS

"The Little Mother," showing a girl making dolls with chiyogami paper. Magazine illustration by Yumeji Takehisa. 1917.

Pattern of stripes in red and green. *Ōnishiki-ban.* Ise-Tatsu Collection. ▶

FOREWORD

In earlier eras, the word *chiyogami* was used as a name for paper decorated with patterns that were considered particularly auspicious. Combinations of cranes and tortoises were popular, because these animals have always served as emblems of long life and happiness. Pine and bamboo trees remain green throughout the coldest weather, while winter-flowering plum trees bloom even when their boughs are decked with snow, giving hope to mankind during the bleakest season of the year. Thus, these three plants were always prized as symbols of good fortune, and they have appeared in countless variations within chiyogami designs.

Chiyogami papers ornamented with these and other auspicious motifs were indispensible accessories for all sorts of happy occasions. This may have some relationship to the name of chiyogami, for the word *chiyo* ("thousand generations") occurs in congratulatory phrases used at such times. Others think that the word may be derived from the name of the Chiyoda Palace, the center of old Edo. Whatever the truth may be, it is at least certain that chiyogami was known in the Edo period (1603–1867). From Kyoto, where it first became popular, it spread to Edo (modern Tokyo) and Osaka. In all three of these cities, it is still being manufactured and sold by a handful of woodblock printers. I am proud to say that my firm, Ise-Tatsu, is one of them. I hope that this book will help to introduce the charm and beauty of chiyogami papers to an ever-widening audience, not only in Japan, but throughout the world.

TATSUGORŌ HIROSE

Chiyogami: An Introduction

In everyday parlance today, the Japanese word *chiyogami* is customarily used to describe several related types of decorative paper intended for consumer use that is printed or otherwise mechanically ornamented with colorful all-over patterns. In many cases, though not necessarily in all, these patterns reflect a more or less "traditional" style, employing themes and color harmonies common to numerous forms of indigenous applied art. Chiyogami papers have formed a small but indispensable part of the daily scene in the urban centers of Japan for at least the past two centuries. They are closely linked to classic Japanese textile arts on the one hand and to traditional graphic design on the other, and it is these relationships, together with the unpretentiously attractive, versatile nature of chiyogami paper itself, to which we might best attribute the enduring popularity of the chiyogami genre.

This brightly colored and tastefully patterned paper is a living legacy of the early modern urban civilization that flourished first in the Kansai area (Kyoto and Osaka) and, somewhat later, in Edo (now Tokyo) during the seventeenth, eighteenth, and nineteenth centuries. While its antecedents and many of its ultimate sources are to be found in the courtly culture of old Kyoto, chiyogami paper as we know it today is an essentially middle-class phenomenon, and may be regarded as a sort of workaday Cinderella sister of the ukiyo-e prints and book illustrations of mid- and late Edo times. Like the landscapes of Hiroshige, the genre prints of Toyokuni and Eisen, or the battle scenes and satires of Kuniyoshi, chiyogami papers were printed by one of the world's first commercially viable forms of multicolor printing: the Japanese woodblock process that was in use as early as the 1760s. There is good reason to suppose that older standards of taste and modes of decoration lingered on in Kyoto and its environs for many years after the mass production of chiyogami hand-printed from woodblocks became commonplace in Edo. In nineteenth-century Edo, however, chiyogami was regularly designed

Fig. 1. Otogi-zoshi cover: fairy-tale book (title: Hachikatsugi) bound in paper decorated with hand-finished designs of origami cranes. Osaka, ca. 1720.

by artists of the ukiyo-e school, issued by their publishers, and purchased by the same relatively well-to-do town-dwelling public that patronized their more ambitious works in the form of prints or illustrated books.

In view of the fact that many orthodox critics of ukiyo-e art have preferred to ignore the existence of applied-art ukiyo-e forms such as chiyogami, it is interesting to note that nineteenth-century chiyogami designs are believed to have been produced not only by nameless commercial artists but also by representative masters of the day, such as Eisen, Hiroshige I, Gyōsai, and Zeshin (Pl. 58). An aura of ambiguity also surrounds the purchasers, for some writers have persisted in stressing the "plebian" nature of chiyogami. This represents a rather excessively romanticized view, for chiyogami was never a product of folk art as such, nor was it meant for the urban poor or others living at the bare subsistence level. Like the handsomely patterned silk fabrics with which it had so much in common stylistically, and like the illustrated books and novels that were its near kindred, chiyogami was created by capable professionals who thoroughly understood their business, and sold as a frankly commercial product. It was bought by consumers of reasonable cultivation and economic substance, who knew what they wanted, and were both willing and able to pay for it—the city dwellers of middle ranks, and especially the wives, children, and elders of the petite bourgeoisie in Edo and other major centers of population.

In addition to these and other areas of similarity between the more ambitious genres of ukiyo-e art on the one hand and chiyogami on the other, there were also significant points of difference. For one thing, unlike its grander kindred among the single-sheet prints, print series, and book illustrations, chiyogami was never intended to point a moral, to adorn a tale, nor even to serve as a focal point for aesthetic appreciation in its own right. From the beginning, it was consciously designed to fulfill a variety of practical purposes, which almost invariably involved transformation into other forms. This

Fig. 2. Decorative book binding with design in chiyogami style by the artist Kiyokata Kaburagi. Tokyo, 1911.

PAPER SIZES:
Ōbōsho-ban (double-size): approximately 54 × 39 cm
Kobōsho-ban (medium-size): approximately 47 × 33 cm
Ōnishiki-ban (half-size): approximately 39 × 27 cm

Chiyogami Predecessors

Note: Items with a plate number preceded by an asterisk belong to the Ise-Tatsu Collection; the remainder belong to the author.

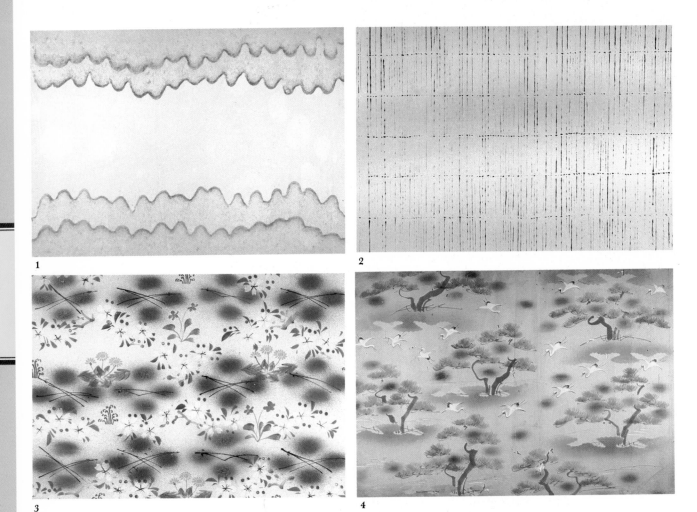

*1. Hand-made paper with wavy design. *Kobōsho-ban*. Mid-Edo period.

*2. Paper with design printed with *sudare* blind. *Kobōsho-ban*. Mid-Edo period.

*3. *Fuki-bokashi* paper: spatter-print design with spring flowers and plants in hand-coloring and stencil printing. *Kobōsho-ban*. Mid-Edo period.

4. *Fuki-bokashi* paper; pine trees and flying cranes. *Kobōsho-ban*. Mid-Edo period.

5

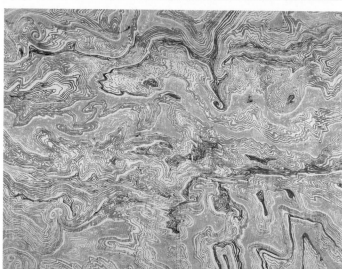

6

*5. *Sumi-nagashi* paper; marbled pattern in ink and colors. *Kobōsho-ban*. Mid-Edo period.
*6. Paper with *sumi-nagashi* ink-marbling pattern imitated in woodblock printing. *Kobōsho-ban*. Mid-Edo period.

functional nature of chiyogami doubtless contributed to its longevity as a genre. At the same time, it has also made it difficult for us to reconstruct its history and development, for the number of extant specimens surviving from earlier ages is not large. It could almost be set up as axiomatic that grandmothers, mothers, and small girls armed with scissors were at once the blessing and the bane of chiyogami: the blessing, because it was their unswerving loyalty through many generations that helped the chiyogami genre to survive to the present day; and the bane, because they left so few intact sheets behind for us to study and observe.

Further, although ukiyo-e prints and paintings are accepted, albeit at times somewhat grudgingly, among Japanese art authorities as suitable for research and museum display, the same respect is not accorded to chiyogami. Despite its obvious visual beauty and sophisticated levels of design, its primary uses were decorative, functional, and commercial, rather than consciously "artistic," and the majority of its consumers were women and children. These circumstances almost automatically put chiyogami (and related forms such as printed games or children's book illustrations) beyond the pale of serious academic consideration, even though many scholars, as well as artists and other persons active in cultural fields, have maintained a fondness for chiyogami from childhood on. Its ephemeral nature has made it very difficult for people to appreciate its long history, while its continuing availability has caused the public at large to take it for granted. In combination, these factors have caused chiyogami to be relegated to a peripheral status among applied art forms dating from the Edo period. It is known, loved, and appreciated by many people in Japan today, but taken seriously only by a minority.

At this point, several specific and concrete questions arise. Just what is chiyogami and how can it be defined? How are we to distinguish it from other types of mechanically decorated paper? There are, after all, countless varieties of such paper being manufactured or sold in Japan today: elegantly designed poem-cards and other calligraphic papers with a history of many centuries, large-format patterned papers of importance in Japanese-style interior decoration, lavish wallpaper after the European manner, and stylish modern wrapping paper to meet all tastes in the preparation of parcels and gifts. What, if any, are the qualities that give chiyogami a distinct character of its own

Fig. 3. Supplement to *Shōjo-no-tomo* ("The Girl's Companion"), vol. 15, no. 1; lithographed board game incorporating chiyogami patterns. Tokyo 1922.

and allow it the status of an independent category among the myriad types of decorative paper currently in use? Many factors are involved, and purists holding particularly rigid views as to what is orthodox, authentic chiyogami and what is not might wish to confine the definition of the word within stricter limits than those suggested here. At the very least, however, and speaking in general terms, it seems safe to say that most specimens of chiyogami share certain common and persistent characteristics, to be found in such aspects as the quality of the paper used, its dimensions, the methods of printing employed, and the uses to which the finished product is put, as well, of course, as in the nature of layout and pictorial content. An examination of some of these areas of similarity may be more useful than a simple definition in understanding chiyogami and the role that it has played in Japanese life.

I. Practical Aspects: Paper Quality, Size, and Printing Techniques

One of the most obvious differences between chiyogami papers and modern patterned products designed for use in packaging is the quality of the paper stock on which they are printed. Even the handsomest and most fancifully designed contemporary gift-wrapping papers are generally meant to be used once and then thrown away. Thus, strength, fineness, and durability are of less importance than immediate visual appeal. By contrast, chiyogami was generally intended for objects for daily use. This meant that it had to be not only attractive, but also supple and durable enough to endure being cut, folded, and pasted. Several types of hand-made Japanese paper were and are traditionally used in quality chiyogami manufacture, but even when modern machine-made papers are used, most manufacturers try to make sure that the resulting chiyogami will still be fine enough for precision folding, and strong enough not to disintegrate when paste is applied to it.

Almost as a matter of course, the dimensions of chiyogami were determined by the sizes of the paper stock used. There is no set rule fixing the measurements of chiyogami, and slight differences may be found even in papers printed at the same time by the same manufacturer. In general, however, there are two accepted formats, of which one is approximately twice the size of the other. The larger of these (ōbōsho-ban) may measure somewhere in the vicinity of 54 by 39 centimeters (21¼ by 15¼ inches), give or take two or three centimeters either way. The half-size variety (ōnishiki-ban) is correspondingly smaller: usually something like 27 by 39 centimeters (10½ by 15¼ inches). A third, medium size (kobōsho-ban), measuring approximately 47 by 33 centimeters (18½ by 13 inches) is also found among specimens dating from earlier stages of chiyogami history. The larger ōbōsho-ban was extremely common from the eighteenth century up to the Meiji era (1868–1912). This format is rare in prints of the ukiyo-e school but is often found among other categories of ornamented paper, including the type known as kara-kami ("Chinese-style paper"). As kara-kami is believed to be a forebear of chiyogami, the continuing use of large-size stock may represent a legacy from the parent form. In some cases, large-format chiyogami papers were designed so that a single sheet could be divided and sold as two half-size sheets. In other instances, the same designs might be available in both formats, with the pattern proportionally reduced to suit the smaller size.

Thus far, the discussion has been limited to chiyogami printed by the classical woodblock process. In recent years, however, the revival of interest in ornamental dolls and figurines made of paper has expanded both the market for woodblock-printed chiyogami and the dimensions of papers sold in department stores and paper shops under the same name but printed by other methods, such as stencil-printing, silk-screen, or offset lithography. Most of these outsize papers were consciously designed to meet the need for materials to be used in new styles of creative doll-making utilizing the basic principles, but not necessarily the forms, of the time-honored paper figures called ane-sama. These were traditionally associated with chiyogami, which makes it only natural that other, related forms of paper for doll-making should be called by the same name. The proportionately lower prices of the newer outsize papers are another reason for their popularity, and most regular purchasers of patterned papers for craft work use both extra-large mechanically printed paper and orthodox chiyogami in the traditional formats. Nonetheless, some people feel that the name chiyogami should be reserved for woodblock-printed papers alone, although, as we shall soon see, other forms of decoration may have preceded it in the early stages of chiyogami history.

Prior to the invention of a seemingly cumbersome but extraordinarily versatile multicolor woodblock-printing technique early in the second half of the eighteenth century, monochrome printing was presumably employed in the manufacture of chiyogami prototypes, along with other yet older forms of embellishment, such as tinting, appliqué, hand-coloring, spatter printing, and stencil painting. Any number of these techniques could be, and frequently were, blended to achieve special effects. In particular, the latter three processes were regularly combined in the production of attractive, gracefully decorated papers known to us collectively as *fuki-bokashi*. Surviving examples often incorporate designs of a pictorial nature closely resembling patterns found in chiyogami (Pls. 3, 4). Some traces from these early stages lingered on into the era of multicolor printing, especially in the Kyoto–Osaka area, their original home, but the newer technique offered greater possibilities for more efficient production and more effective color work at less cost, and it was soon adapted to the manufacture of patterned paper.

With the adoption of imported mechanical printing techniques during the Meiji era, woodblock printing in multicolor and monochrome rapidly gave way to other methods on most fronts of the publishing industry. It was retained for a time in a few specialized areas—many literary works of the 1890s combined linotyped texts with woodblock frontispieces, probably because woodblock printing yielded results that were aesthetically far superior to the color-work possibilities offered by imported mechanical processes prior to the naturalization of offset lithography. In addition, woodblock printing also remained in use for certain peripheral genres of publishing, especially where no imported equivalent had been introduced to disturb the status quo. These included several minor but interesting and historically significant types of graphic material, such as the *senja-fuda* ("thousand-shrine ticket") cards, which provided an artistic outlet for the all-too-human desire to leave one's mark upon public buildings and chiyogami. The *senja-fuda* cards are luxury items, usually designed and made to order for coteries of collectors, but woodblock-printed chiyogami continues to be sold over the counter to the general public in answer to a limited but stable consumer demand. Thus, it is possible to regard the humble chiyogami as one of the few actual survivors (as distinguished from later revivals and facsimiles) of woodblock printing in the

Fig. 4. Chiyogami book jacket made by a postwar nursing student for one of her textbooks. Tokyo, *ca.* 1945.

Fig. 5. Decorative wrappers of chiyogami of a limited-edition magazine for connoisseurs; *Ōdomo*, nos. 2, 4, and 7. Tokyo, 1918–20. Chiyogami by Ise-Tatsu.

ukiyo-e tradition, which has gone on fulfilling its original functions along an unbroken line of transmission from the Edo period to the present.

II. The Uses of Chiyogami

Even more than paper quality, dimensions, or printing methods, it is these "original functions"—the manifold domestic and commercial uses of chiyogami—that influenced its development as a distinct category of graphic design. During Edo and Meiji times and even more recently, chiyogami was habitually employed in the manufacture of many articles necessary, useful, or desirable in everyday life: boxes, cases, folders, envelopes, and other containers large and small for countless purposes and all occasions, ornamental gift wrappings, decorations and other objects for use at annual festivals or other auspicious occasions, and personal accessories such as ladies' portable cosmetics holders, which were often lined with chiyogami. Chiyogami served as material for book wrappers and covers, and in the repairing of books; late Edo and early Meiji publishers frequently used attractively patterned papers for the back covers of novels or picture books and, while most of these were specially printed for the purpose, some of them may also have been related to chiyogami or chiyogami design.

Chiyogami was widely employed in origami paper folding; today, manufacturers regularly dignify ordinary patterned origami paper printed by offset lithography with the name of chiyogami. Woodblock-printed chiyogami found a place in other crafts and in toy-making among both professionals and amateurs and among adults and children alike; as we have already noted, one of the most typical and charming traditional uses for chiyogami was in the construction of costumes and hair ornaments for the elaborate three-dimensional paper figurines known in the Tokyo dialect as *ane-sama*, "elder sister" dolls. These dolls ultimately stemmed from a simpler type of figure found in many variations throughout much of Japan and in continental Asia as well. Earlier and more primitive versions utilized natural materials, but the classic forms of *ane-sama* as they are commonly remembered today were usually made of paper alone. Their early history is yet to be written, but they were apparently known in urban households of Japan at least as early as the late eighteenth century.

As was the case with origami, it is probably no coincidence that *ane-sama* began to flourish at a time when ornamental paper was increasingly regarded as a necessity; in return, the influence of *ane-sama* upon chiyogami was probably always much greater than has generally been realized, even before the postwar doll-making revival. One direct result was the enormous number of miniature adaptations from standard all-over fabric patterns, such as stripes, plaids, dots, or other geometric designs, and floral scatter prints. Because of their relative monotony and lack of visual impact, only a few of these patterns are depicted in this book, but they comprise one of the largest and most important categories of chiyogami—doubtless because of their indispensability in doll-making. There was also an interesting related genre, midway between chiyogami and woodblock-printed broadsides for children, that went several steps further than ordinary chiyogami by offering the user four or five different pre-assembled *ane-sama* costumes, economically combined within a single sheet. This "super-chiyogami" has recently been revived with success by Senrei Sekioka, a leading Tokyo woodblock-printing specialist.

Due to their perishable nature, early examples of *ane-sama* are, if anything, even scarcer than uncut sheets of old chiyogami. Thanks to their presence in many book illustrations, prints, and paintings of domestic scenes, however, it is possible for us to gain some idea of what they looked like and how they were made and used. A comparison of these pictures shows that *ane-sama* figures in the style traditionally associated with the Tokyo area have changed very little during the past two centuries. Today, *ane-sama* are no longer used as toys, but many types of paper figurines in both classical and creative styles are favorites with amateur craftspeople and schools of doll-making, so that the traditional symbiotic relationship between *ane-sama* and chiyogami is once more in a flourishing state of health.

The visual possibilities of chiyogami have also attracted the attention of modern graphic artists working in collage. In prewar Japan, the eminent creative print designers Takeo Takei and Shigeru Hatsuyama, among others, made good use of chiyogami in collage designs for books and children's magazines. Chiyogami and other patterned papers from Japan also played

Fig. 6. Cover design for April 1902 issue of *Shōjo-kai* ("Girls' World"), incorporating pictures of *ane-sama* figures. Tokyo, 1902.

17

important roles in a famous series of collage-illustrated picture books (*Peter's Chair* and its sequels) by the postwar American artist Ezra Jack Keats.

While these and other uses of chiyogami usually involved its transformation into other forms, there were always people who purchased chiyogami for a purpose less destructive, if less creative—collectors of all ages who liked to own and enjoy chiyogami simply as a visual treat, with no immediate intentions of using it. Several serious adult collectors of chiyogami have also left valuable records of their collections in book form. The oldest example presently known is a quarto album published in Kyoto in 1919, which introduces the early chiyogami owned by one connoisseur in collotype illustrations; although it contains no text, it is important as the first book (apart from dealers' catalogues) to attempt to reevaluate chiyogami ephemera as an independent genre of graphic art.

There were some adults who collected chiyogami for professional reasons: designers, silk merchants, dyers, and other members of the fashion industry in search of reference material for patterns and color-harmony possibilities. Many children and adolescents collected chiyogami with the same enthusiasm that others devoted to insects or stamps; during World War II, some even took their precious collections with them when they were evacuated to remote country districts away from the danger of bomb raids. Adults and children, amateurs and professionals alike, these collectors deserve to be thanked for seeing to it that some examples of chiyogami were preserved for the enjoyment of future generations, including our own.

Whatever the aims of these consumers of chiyogami, we may be sure that all of them were attracted by its visual appeal based on content and design, topics significant enough to deserve a section of their own.

III. Visual Aspects: Theme, Content, and Composition

Central to any study of chiyogami, because most immediately obvious, are the twin aspects of content and composition—the accepted themes, patterns, and pictorial motifs found in chiyogami, along with the standard conventions of layout determining their arrangement within the two-dimensional microcosm formed by a sheet of paper. Together, these twin elements constitute the basic visual vocabulary and grammar of chiyogami design. As we have already noted, chiyogami makes use of thematic elements common to many other time-honored industrial crafts of Japan, and it is linked by especially close ties to the world of textile arts. This does not mean that chiyogami papers merely ape the patterns found in Japanese silks or cottons, for chiyogami has its own uses, conventions, and requirements, which naturally differ from those of fabrics. Rather, it might be more accurate to say that many chiyogami designs represent cleverly handled rephrasings of traditional Japanese fabric styles and idioms, adapted to a greatly reduced scale and to the limitations imposed by a rectangular format.

As a result, miniature reworkings of classical geometric and abstract textile patterns abound within chiyogami. These share pride of place with other popular fabric-decoration motifs, such as themes derived from plants and natural phenomena, from the symbolism of the four seasons, and from toys, household goods, and the paraphernalia of everyday life. Plum-pine-and-bamboo combinations, peonies, chrysanthemums, open fans, and other auspicious motifs appropriate to festive and ceremonial events are also found in quantities more than sufficient to emphasize the practical nature of chiyogami and the many domestic functions that it fulfilled on congratulatory occasions. It comes as no surprise to find chiyogami designs derived from specific annual festivals of the traditional calendar year, such as the New Year season of early January, the Doll Festival on the third of March (Pl. 111), and the Star Festival on the seventh of July (Pl. 83), for all of these provided excuses for considerable consumption of ornamental paper.

Another fruitful source of thematic material was provided by the world of literature and the stage. Between them, the great classic novel known as *Genji Monogatari* ("The Tale of Genji") and the Kabuki drama could probably be said to account for at least one-tenth of all chiyogami designs, while proverbs, much-loved fairy tales, and classical poetry are also represented. Chinese characters and the home-grown Japanese phonetic syllabary scripts known as *kana* appear in many guises, and there was at least one successful chiyogami adaptation of the Roman alphabet—a handsomely stylized version somewhat redolent of the mature art deco manner of the versatile artist and illustrator Ryūshi Kawabata during the 1930s (Pl. 91, at right). In addition to literary works themselves, the vehicles of literary expression have also been incorporated into many chiyogami patterns: calligraphic poem-cards, printed pages, and literary playing cards from such games as the Alphabet Proverbs or the Hundred Poets are often found in all-over scatter and collage-style designs.

Though chiyogami itself belongs to the spheres of printing and publishing, this kinship does not, of course, give it a monopoly on pictorial themes of a literary nature. Like the other types of ornament already introduced, motifs related to books, printing, poetry, and the theater have continued to play important roles in fabric decor from the Edo period to the present, and some designs were doubtless taken into chiyogami by way of textile dyers' pattern-books. Themes from the classic prose romance known as *Ise Monogatari* ("Tales of Ise"), for example, are common in Japanese textiles and costume design. When depictions of the Iris Bridge at Yatsuhashi, the Ivy Path, the seagulls on the Sumida River, the Tatsuta River in autumn, or other subjects from *Ise Monogatari* occur in chiyogami patterns, the chances are that they are not conscious references to the story of the courtier-poet Narihira and his many loves, but simply chiyogami adaptations of attractive textile motifs that happened to be derived from the tale.

Where drama and the literature of the theatre are concerned, however, the case is somewhat different, for themes relating to the stage were intentionally employed by both textile and chiyogami designers alike—not only in a general sense but often with specific reference to a particular play, actor, or individual role. During the heyday of the Kabuki drama as a seminal force in the cultural life of urban middle-class Japan, there were sound economic reasons behind this wholesale adoption of theatrical motifs into books and other commercial items such as textiles and chiyogami: late-Edo-period and Meiji-era consumers delighted in purchasing goods associated with their favorite actors, or with plays that were the talk of the town. Publishers of chiyogami were quick to take advantage of this amiable weakness on the part of their customers, and the result was a tempting array of theatrical chiyogami designs. Some of these were frankly taken over from fabrics and the fashion industry, while others were independent chiyogami adaptations of motifs from the world of the stage.

Examples of chiyogami from the first category often look like nothing so much as miniature paper versions of textiles regularly seen on the stage or in the greenrooms of Kabuki theaters. With chiyogami representing the latter type, themes borrowed from the drama tend to be more indirect and less immediately obvious; they are not always easy to recognize without some prior background knowledge of the Kabuki milieu. For example, a pleasant all-over design that appears purely visual and not in the least literary may nonetheless turn out to be a pictorial allusion to an acting family or a scene from the Kabuki stage. Thus, a semi-abstract treatment of waves and a pine-girt seacoast, with a superimposed pattern of phoenix feathers, epitomizes the dance-drama *Hagoromo* ("The Feathered Robe"), taken into the Kabuki repertory from a Noh play based upon a fairy-tale theme (Pl. 34). Another design, of falling cherry blossoms and hand-drums scattered seemingly at random across a blue-and-white checkered ground, clearly alludes to a spectacular scene from the historical drama *Yoshitsune Senbon-zakura* ("Yoshitsune's Flight to Mt. Yoshino") and would be recognized as such by connoisseurs of Kabuki, even without the descriptive title that accompanies it. Many more examples could be listed, and it is probable that yet others remain unidentified, simply because the theatrical topics to which they refer have faded from the popular memory.

While themes from *The Tale of Genji* do not, perhaps, occur with the frequency of those derived from the stage, they are nonetheless very common indeed, and their close relationship with chiyogami probably dates from an era prior to the earliest appearance of theatrical motifs within the genre. Their history as chiyogami decor is not only long but also continuous, extending from the eighteenth century to the present day. In an annotated catalogue of paper varieties believed to date from 1728, the earliest known reference to chiyogami appears in a section devoted to other, presumably related, forms of patterned paper. One of its immediate neighbors in the same section is called by the name of *Genji-e*—literally, "Genji pictures"—but otherwise unidentified. As the paper historian Yasutaka Morita suggests, this may simply mean painted battle scenes depicting the medieval wars between the two rival clans known as Genji and Heike. If, however, it refers to paper decorated with motifs from *The Tale of Genji* (as seems more likely in a book published

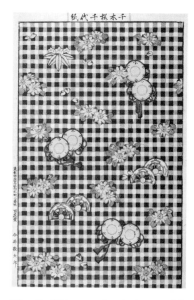

Fig. 7. Chiyogami design with motifs based on the Kabuki play *Yoshitsune Senbon-zakura*. Tokyo, *ca.* 1890.

in early eighteenth-century Kyoto), this indicates that *Genji Monogatari* themes were already in use during the earliest stages of chiyogami development and may even be older than chiyogami itself.

Many Genji-derived chiyogami designs tend to be emblematic rather than representational, with symbolic devices borrowed from one or the other of two aristocratic pastimes taking the place of pictorial images. The first and older of these is the game of shell-matching, in which players sought to assemble the separated halves of clamshells into pairs. The shells were usually elegantly gilded and ornamented with graceful designs based upon works of classical Japanese literature. This amusement was particularly popular from the late middle ages to the eighteenth century, and it probably influenced the development of classical Japanese pastimes played with paired sets of cards, such as the Hundred Poets and the *Genji Monogatari* verse game, so that shell-matching itself gradually came to be linked in the popular mind with the fictional Prince Genji and his world. The same association was extended to pictorial representations of decorated shells or clamshell outlines used in scatter patterns. Two examples of typical shell-outline chiyogami designs appear in this book, in Plates 38 and 84.

The second Genji-related pastime to leave its mark upon chiyogami design was an incense-guessing game enjoyed in aristocratic circles from the time of its invention in the seventeenth century. From five different varieties of incense, used both singly and in ingenious assortments, fifty-two arbitrary combinations were determined: the object of the game was the correct identification of the particular combinations. Each of the fifty-two sets was called after one of the fifty-four chapters of *The Tale of Genji* (the first and last chapters excepted), and represented by its own symbol: an abstract, streamlined pattern of five slender, vertical rectangles arranged to indicate the number and order of the incense varieties used in a given combination.

These devices soon began to appear in many cultural fields far outside the bounds of the rarified world of incense appreciation; they were heartily welcomed by designers in numerous areas of applied art, including the textile industry, as well as by publishers of eductional material, games, books, and prints (including, of course, chiyogami). As a part of their literary education, young people, especially girls, learned to identify the symbols, which

Fig. 8. Home-made board game and wrapper; a version of *jurokumusashi* made from *Genji-kō* chiyogami. Edo (Tokyo), *ca.* 1830–50.

were freely used as outright synonyms for the names of the Genji chapters they represented. In early nineteenth-century Kyoto, Osaka, or Edo, to anyone with reasonable pretensions to literacy, the symbol 𝍌 was not simply a curious comblike conglomeration of vertical lines, but an immediately recognizable ideograph that read *Hana-chiru Sato* ("The Village of Falling Flowers"), the title of the eleventh chapter of *The Tale of Genji*. A hint of the original source lingered on in the name *Genji-kō* ("Genji incense"), which remained in use as a generic term for the incense-game emblems, individually or en masse, but the emblems themselves achieved independent status as alternative titles for the Genji chapters quite apart from the game. Although their individual meanings are no longer common knowledge, some of these symbols are still in evidence in daily life in Japan today, in Kabuki costumes and stage decor, in the patterns of textiles for kimono and yukata fashions, and in trademarks for a variety of businesses, from cosmetic manufacturers to bakeries. The *Hana-chiru Sato* mark was even used as a logo by an otherwise unknown publisher who produced an unusual series of chiyogami with an art deco flavor, presumably during the 1920s (Pls. 63–66).

Despite (or perhaps because of) their simplicity of form, the Genji emblems lent themselves to a number of different treatments within chiyogami. All of the symbols might be marshaled in orderly sequences, sometimes with small pictorial glosses added to increase the variety of the design, suggest the topics of the fifty-two chapters with emblems, and fill in the visual blanks left by the first and fifty-fourth chapters. Alternatively, the emblems might simply be sprinkled at random in white across a colored ground. Some of the most interesting Genji chiyogami patterns also combine shell-outlines with Genji-incense symbols, as does the patterned paper used in the back covers of some volumes of the famous parody *Inaka Genji* ("The Rustic Genji") by Ryūtei Tanehiko, a bestseller of the 1830s. As fragments of the same paper are occasionally found in other formats, it seems reasonable to assume that it was also issued and sold as chiyogami, thus allowing publishers to reap even greater profits from the popularity of the book.

Chiyogami designers made lavish use of the rich traditional Japanese reservoir of design and symbol, but they also paid close attention to current fashions, and attractive or newsworthy topics of the day. Such topical themes were

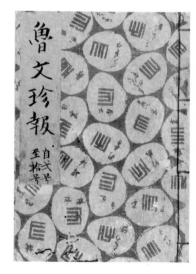

Fig. 9. *Genji-kō* chiyogami cover, presumably home-made, for a Meiji-period magazine. Tokyo, *ca.* 1890 (chiyogami may date from several decades earlier).

already being welcomed by consumers in Edo times; the previously mentioned patterns referring to popular Kabuki actors, and the new Genji chiyogami produced at the height of the "Rustic Genji" craze are cases in point. Meiji-era chiyogami designs of Japanese flags and lanterns are doubtless oblique references to such events as the promulgation of the Meiji Constitution in 1889 or the victories in the Sino-Japanese and Russo-Japanese wars, occasions that were celebrated with lantern parades more or less equivalent to the old-fashioned American torchlight processions on election days.

Some patterns from the 1920s and 1930s make much use of wooden *kokeshi* dolls and other rustic toys; on the surface they look like pure expressions of traditional thematic material. But since depictions of such regional items are rare in earlier chiyogami, these patterns probably reflect the fashion for collecting rural toys that flourished among nostalgic city people in Japan of the Taishō and early Shōwa eras. At the same time, the legitimate interests of children were not neglected: at a very early stage in his career, Mickey Mouse himself made at least one appearance in woodblock-printed chiyogami (Pl. 74). In other chiyogami designs from the twenties and thirties, toy cars, toy trains, and stylishly whimsical imported dolls abound, while depictions of steeple-shaped radios, art deco hair ornaments, and telephones demonstrate that the chiyogami of the decades between the wars was still a living tradition able to assimilate new ideas and changing styles.

By contrast with the exuberant richness, color, and variety of thematic content found in chiyogami, the topics of layout and composition do not appear very promising at first glance. Nonetheless, chiyogami composition had its own definite rules and conventions, which were crucial in determining the relative failure or success of any given design. Since chiyogami was primarily decorative rather than representational, its designers had little need to concern themselves with questions of depth, perspective, or complex spatial relationships. Instead, they were obliged to grapple with other problems, of equal or greater complexity.

First and most important, they were expected to produce designs possessed of interest and appeal on two coexisting levels. It was not enough for chiyogami merely to be attractive enough to catch the eye of consumers in its primal four-cornered, two-dimensional state, before it left the shop: it also

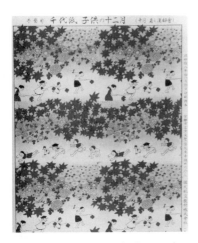

Fig. 10. Lithographed wartime chiyogami; design incorporates a popular character created by the cartoonist Ryūichi Yokoyama. Kyoto, 1943.

had to live up to the expectations of purchasers who bought it for the express purpose of re-making it into some other object altogether. While it was not so difficult for a well-trained commercial artist to fulfill either of these conditions independently of one another, the question of providing for both of them at once, and in the same design, was less easily answered.

In the second place, chiyogami designers were required to keep a large established repertory of theme, pictorial motif, and symbol always at their fingertips, and to understand what kinds of layout, and what proportions, were most suitable in adapting them to the format of chiyogami. They also had to develop the invaluable ability to strike an appropriate balance between tradition, originality, and common sense, so that their designs were familiar enough to answer to ordinary purposes, and unusual enough to provoke consumer interest, but, at the same time, not so exaggerated, nor so divorced from practical considerations, as to prove useless for their proper functions. In many instances, "name" artists might break all the rules with impunity, and still rest assured of reasonable sales, not necessarily because they produced better chiyogami, but because of their fame among the public at large: the chiyogami designs by Yumeji Takehisa (Pls. 67–72) and Sumio Kawakami (Pls. 81, 93, 109) could be cited as cases in point. Commercial artists who specialized in chiyogami could not afford to take such extravagant chances, for the fate of their work was determined not by name value, but by quality alone.

The number of different formats found in chiyogami is larger than might be expected. Many chiyogami sheets, including some abstract geometric designs and small-scale scatter patterns, have no governing direction, and may be looked at (or cut) from any angle. Others have a definite top and bottom; many examples appear among the plates illustrating this book. Several gradations may be found in the range between these two extremes. One of the most interesting and typical conventions of chiyogami design is borrowed from *kara-kami* layout—the principle known in Japanese as *okuri*, or "sending on." In chiyogami specimens of this group, the patterns of parallel edges are designed to correspond perfectly with one another, so that the top and bottom edges (or the left and right) can be matched to avoid waste, or to make it easier to link several sheets in a large overall design. Much of the best and most conscientiously designed chiyogami incorporates this principle; the striking series of double-size chiyogami believed to have been designed for the long-established Tokyo paper dealer Haibara by the Meiji artist Gyokushō Kawabata (Pl. 35) provides us with many ingenious examples of *okuri*, as does the ambitious series of handsome half-size paper which Shōko Suzuki produced during the 1930s for the woodblock printer Senrei Sekioka I (Pls. 83, 98).

In every era of chiyogami production, from the early nineteenth century up to the 1940s, there was always a slowly evolving, relatively stable core of stock motifs, themes, and accepted composition styles, which maintained their popularity because of their familiarity and general usefulness. Some of them were based on textile patterns, while others were deliberately executed to serve as chiyogami designs. This core of old, established motifs was supplemented by a fluctuating current of other, equally attractive designs that were constantly developing in accordance with changing fashions and topics of the day. The vitality of chiyogami as a genre was strengthened by this successful combination of classicism and conventionality with timeliness, and the ability to adapt to new circumstances.

Due to its status as an applied-art product intended for commercial sale, chiyogami was obliged to meet yet other exacting conditions. It was not meant for art critics, nor exclusively for professional aesthetes, but for the general public, which can be sterner in its dictates than any self-conscious arbiter of elegance. In order to succeed in the struggle for a market, a chiyogami design had to offer a reasonable prospect of suitability for the normal practical uses to which chiyogami was put. It had to be attractive enough to catch the attention of prospective purchasers, but, at the same time, it dared not go beyond the limits of taste that they understood and could accept, nor could its cost exceed the prices that they were willing to pay.

When chiyogami is regarded in this light, it becomes easier for us to understand that the extraordinary visual beauty, sophistication, and verve of many chiyogami designs are not only remarkable in their own right. They are also a testimonial to the high levels of taste and discernment characterizing the ordinary Japanese consumers, of all ages, both sexes, and many walks of life, who enjoyed and appreciated them.

IV. Then and Now: Chiyogami in Edo Times and Today

The early history of chiyogami is nearly as obscure as the original meaning of the name by which it is known. Specimens of old chiyogami from years prior to the mid-nineteenth century are not common, and only rarely dated; despite much conjecture, it has so far proven all but impossible to ascertain how and why chiyogami evolved, or what early examples looked like. The name is found in mid-eighteenth-century documents, and can be traced back with reasonable certainty to 1728. In that year, the Kyoto savant Seichiku Kimura is believed to have compiled an annotated list of paper varieties in use at the time; in a section devoted to patterned and ornamental papers, including the previously mentioned "Genji pictures," the name *chiyogami* appears, albeit with a gloss giving the alternate reading of *sendaishi*. At that time, the word may not have had precisely the same meaning that it has today, but we can be fairly certain that it referred to some sort of attractive paper generically related to modern chiyogami.

Mid-Edo-period prototypes of chiyogami included categories such as marbled paper (*sumi-nagashi*, or "ink-flow" paper; Pl. 5) and the previously introduced spatter-printed paper (*fuki-bokashi*), which often incorporated hand-printed embellishments. Another even more closely related variety was *kōzei* paper (named for a noted calligrapher of Heian times), characterized by appealing all-over patterns woodblock-printed in monochrome colors. Since *kō-zei* paper was used in binding books for children, it bore a marked functional resemblance both to the later chiyogami and to the famous floral-patterned "Dutch paper" imported from Germany for similar purposes by John Newbury and other publishers of typical eighteenth-century British children's books. Further early collaterals of chiyogami to employ printing included paper with patterns in pearl-grey (*tsuki-kage*, or "moon-shadows"), calligraphic papers known as *e-bangiri* and *e-bōsho*, as well as the many varieties of "Chinese paper" (*kara-kami*), which were introduced previously.

Judging from comparisons with these related types of paper and from secondary evidence in documentary sources, the earliest forms of chiyogami proper are thought to have come into use among aristocratic circles in the ancient capital of Kyoto at some time not much later than about 1700. The

Fig. 11. Chiyogami prototype; kozei paper with wood-block-printed designs in monochrome; cover of a picture book for children. Kyoto, mid-eighteenth century.

Fig. 12. Gilt-patterned endpaper of a German devotional book for children. Halle, 1753.

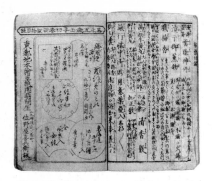

Fig. 13. Page from an Edo-period novel with publisher's advertisements for chiyogami from Edo and Kyoto. Edo (Tokyo), 1852.

next significant advances in the evolution of chiyogami probably resulted from the technical breakthrough in color printing in the last half of the eighteenth century and the marked rise in the economic and cultural power of the urban middle classes. In books aimed primarily at middle-class readers, advertisements for chiyogami become increasingly common during the earlier decades of the nineteenth century. Advertisements published in Edo often list two general categories of chiyogami: paper imported from Kyoto, which was presumably more expensive and therefore more fashionable, as well as a home-grown variety.

From that time to this, chiyogami production has been continuously carried on in both Tokyo and Kyoto, as well as in Osaka. Although the number of manufacturers of chiyogami is no more than a small percentage of what it must have been in Edo or Meiji times, there are still at least ten printers and paper dealers that make or handle quality woodblock chiyogami today. Specialist Tokyo producers include Ise-Tatsu, Haibara, Sekioka, Kobayashi, and Iwase, while Miyamoto and a few other printers were still issuing woodblock chiyogami in recent years. The appealing chiyogami series issued in the early 1940s by the print gallery Go-Hachi did not survive the war years; in its place, however, the firm has revived some unusual designs originally published in 1935 by the noted creative print artist Sumio Kawakami. In Kyoto, chiyogami is available from the old, established firm of Sakurai-ya and the specialist printer Igai Hanga-dō; another Kyoto firm, Pyonpyon-dō, was active up until a few years ago. Although its predecessors Yanagi-ya and Momiji-ya are no longer in existence, the Osaka printer Tenichi-dō continues to produce woodblock-printed chiyogami that is popular among doll-making enthusiasts throughout the nation.

A more detailed discussion of the artistic and social history of chiyogami development from late Edo times to the present must await a further opportunity. The plates, which appear in roughly chronological order, are fully able to speak for themselves; it is hoped that they will aid readers in discovering and appreciating the little-known but attractive and thought-provoking world of chiyogami.

Late Edo Period (1800–1867)

7

7. Chrysanthemums in colors and gauffrage. *Kobōsho-ban. Ca.* 1840.

8. Peonies on yellow ground. *Kobōsho-ban*. 1858.

9. Peonies on dark blue ground. *Kobōsho-ban*.

8

9

10

10. Peonies on dark blue ground. *Kobōsho-ban*.

11. Cherry blossoms. *Ko-bōsho-ban*. 1866.

12. Cherry or peach blossoms. *Ko-bōsho-ban*.

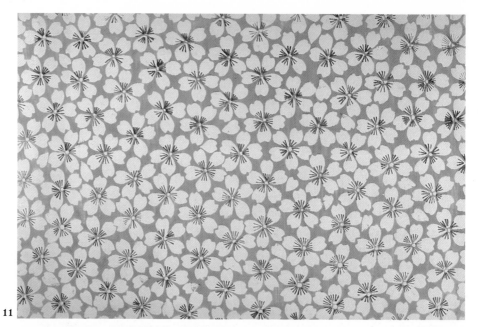

11

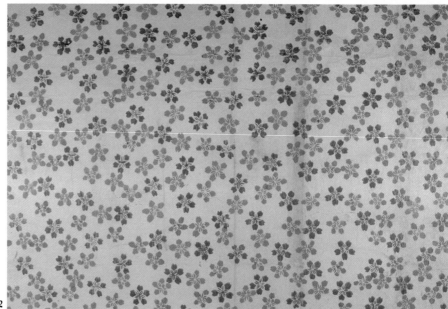

12

13. Stylized phoenixes in annular form. *Kobōsho-ban.*

14. Auspicious emblems. *Kobōsho-ban.*

15. Peonies and flying phoenixes. *Kobōsho-ban.*

13

14

15

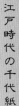

16

16. Incense emblems related to *The Tale of Genji*. *Kobōsho-ban*. 1857.

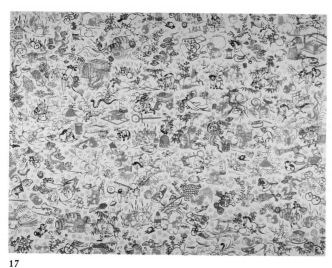

17

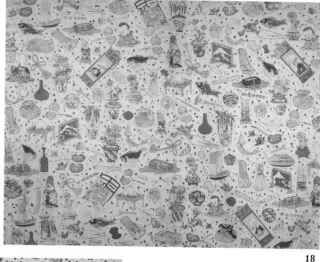

18

19

*17. The twelve animals of the Chinese zodiac. *Kobōsho-ban*. 1855.

*18. Scatter pattern of flowers and emblems of good fortune. *Kobōsho-ban*. 1858.

19. Emblems of the Five Annual Observances: the New Year Festival (January), the Doll Festival (March), the Iris Festival (May), the Star Festival (July), and the Chrysanthemum Festival (September). *Kobōsho-ban*.

20. Design of crests of Kabuki actors (fragment).

20

21

22

21. Kitchen utensils and household implements; chiyogami design in the style of an educational print for children. *Kobōsho-ban.*

*22. Potted plants; containers are decorated with actors' crests. *Kobōsho-ban.*

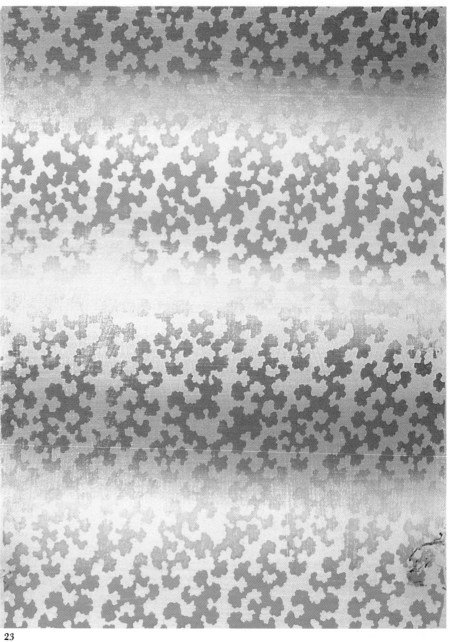

23. Abstract design in red and green. *Ōbōsho-ban*.

23

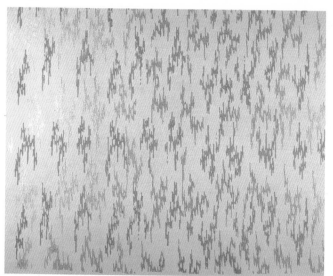

24

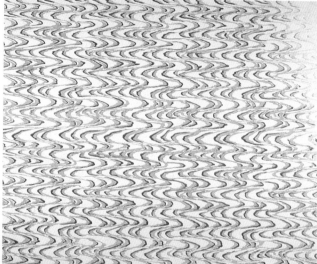

25

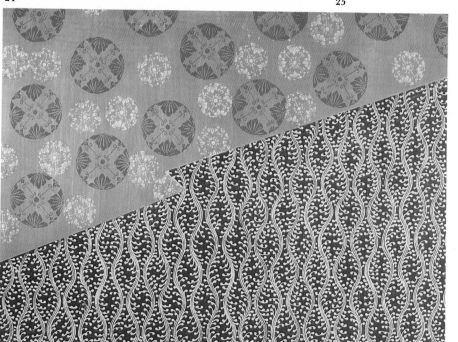

26

*24. Abstract design in red and silver. Ōbōsho-ban.

*25. Stylized water pattern in light and dark blue with shading at left side. Ōbōsho-ban.

26. Patterned paper combining two contrasting designs. Kobōsho-ban.

39

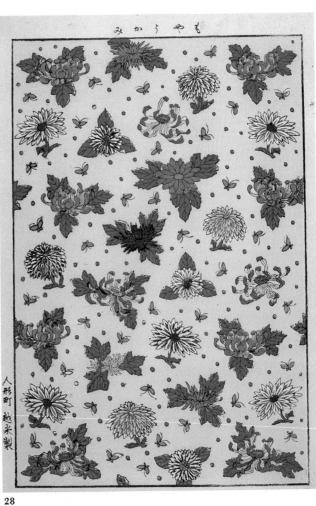

27

28

27. Spider chrysanthemums on pale blue ground. *Ōnishiki-ban.*

28. Assorted chrysanthemums and butterflies on yellow ground. *Ōnishiki-ban.*

29

29. Illustration from a Kyoto pattern book containing several designs later appearing in the chiyogami format. 1894.

***30**. Flowers and maple leaves on black ground; design may be based on the illustration shown in the previous plate. *Ōbōsho-ban*.

30

31

32

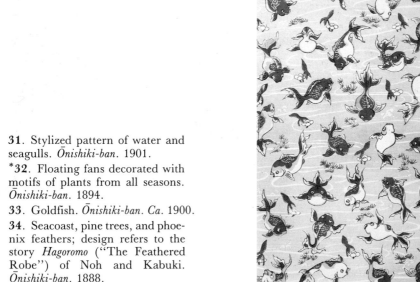

33

34

31. Stylized pattern of water and seagulls. *Ōnishiki-ban*. 1901.

***32**. Floating fans decorated with motifs of plants from all seasons. *Ōnishiki-ban*. 1894.

33. Goldfish. *Ōnishiki-ban. Ca.* 1900.

34. Seacoast, pine trees, and phoenix feathers; design refers to the story *Hagoromo* ("The Feathered Robe") of Noh and Kabuki. *Ōnishiki-ban*. 1888.

35

35. Leaves and pine needles on scarlet ground; designed by
Gyokushō Kawabata. *Ōbōsho-ban*.

36

37

36. Plum blossoms, orchids, chrysanthemums, and bamboo: the Four Noble Plants of Chinese tradition. *Ōnishiki-ban*.

37. Flowers of the four seasons in a stylized wave pattern. *Ōnishiki-ban*. 1887.

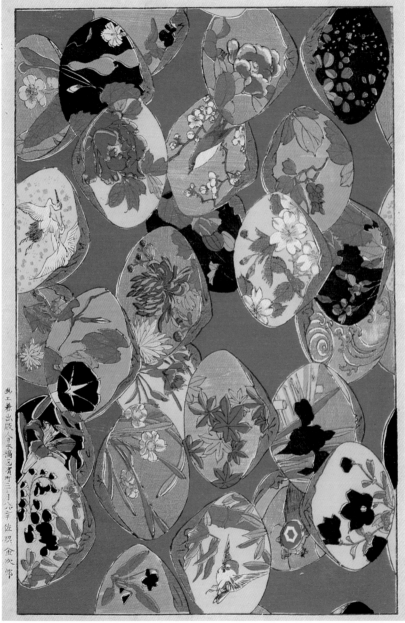

38

38. Shells ornamented with designs of flowers and birds from all seasons. *Ōnishiki-ban*.

39

39. Fukusuke: comic, large-headed figures that are playful emblems of good luck. *Kobōsho-ban*.

40

40. O-fuku: female counterparts of Fukusuke. *Kobōsho-ban*.

41. Peony blossoms and phoenixes on latticed ground; designed by Yoshifuji, a famous pupil of Kuniyoshi. *Ōnishiki-ban*. 1881.

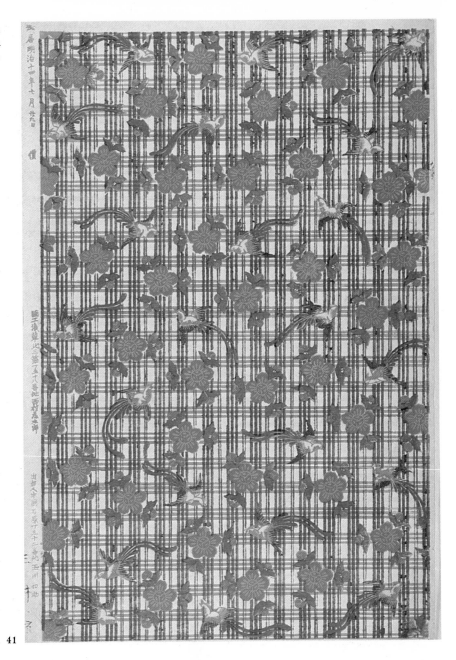

41

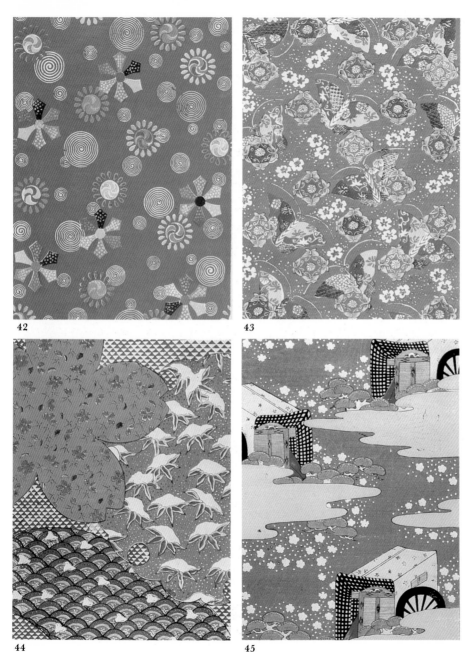

42. Abstract whirligig and windmill design on purple ground. *Ōnishiki-ban*.

43. Stylized butterflies and cherry blossoms on purple ground. *Ōnishiki-ban*.

44. Stylized large-scale pattern of snow-covered bamboo leaves, waves, and outsize cherry blossom on diapered purple and white ground. *Ōnishiki-ban*.

45. *Genji-guruma*: classical ox-drawn carriages with stylized cloud patterns, pine trees, and flowers on purple ground. *Ōnishiki-ban*. 1902.

42

43

44

45

46. Cherry blossoms and chrysanthemum leaves on navy blue ground. *Ōnishiki-ban*.

***47**. Stylized trellis with convolvulus vines and blossoms. *Ōnishiki-ban*.

48. Coltsfoot plants; leaves are ornamented with geometric and flower-and-bird designs; pattern is matched at top and bottom edges. *Ōbōsho-ban*.

46

47

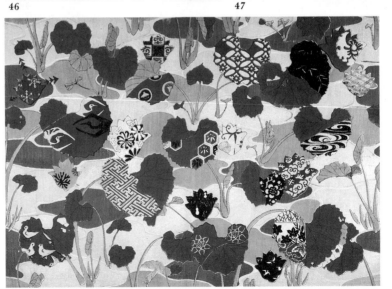

48

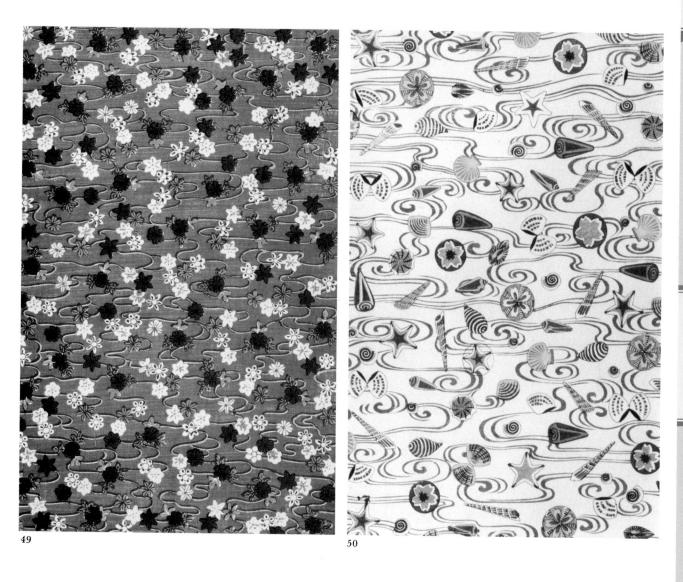

49. Clematis blossoms and stylized waves on red ground. *Ōnishiki-ban*.

50. Seashells and stylized waves. *Ōnishiki-ban*.

51. Shells and folded paper cranes on ground divided diagonally into three sections. *Ōnishiki-ban*. 1902.

52. Cherry blossoms and balancing toys (*yajirobei*); pattern may be a simile for spring flower-viewing parties. *Ōnishiki-ban*.

53. Pine trees and wisteria blossoms. *Ōbōsho-ban*.

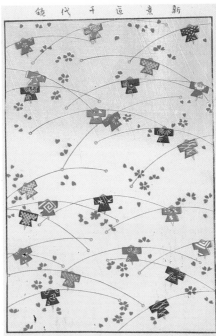

51

52

53

54

*54. All-over design of camellia blossoms; pattern is matched at top and bottom edges. *Ōbōsho-ban.*
55. Blue and pale pink hydrangeas on red ground. *Ōnishiki-ban.*
56. Grapevines on blue ground. *Ōnishiki-ban.*

55

56

57

*57. Round fans for summer use decorated with flower patterns incorporating shading and gauffrage. *Ōnishiki-ban*.

*58. Decorated fans on ground of stylized waves and blossoms; designed by Zeshin Shibata. *Ōbōsho-ban*.

59. Decorated fans scattered at random across red ground; pattern is matched at top and bottom edges. *Ōnishiki-ban*.

58

59

55

60. Music for the New Year: strings and bridges for the shamisen. *Ōnishiki-ban.*

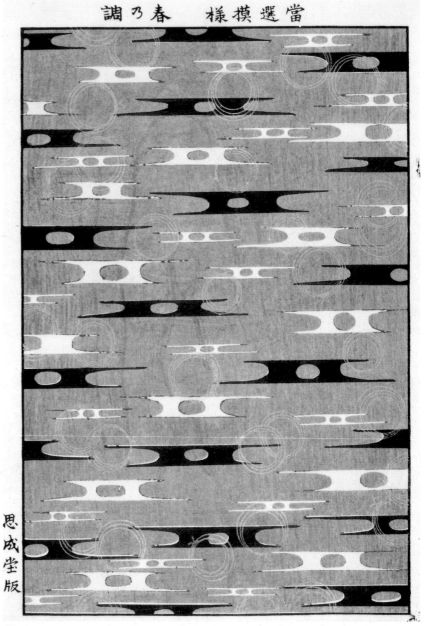

Taishō Period (1912–26)

61

62

61. The twelve animals of the Chinese zodiac; evenly spaced roundels on black ground. *Ōnishiki-ban*.

62. Stylized emblems of good fortune within "tortoiseshell" hexagons amid plum blossoms and snowflakes on black ground. *Ōnishiki-ban*.

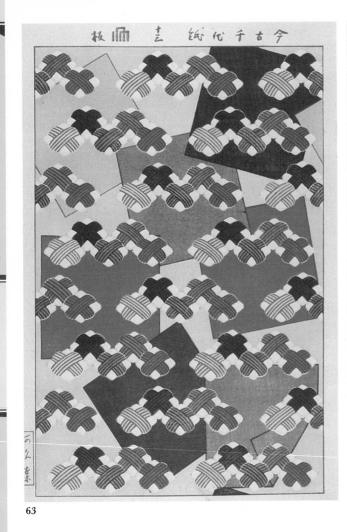

63

64

63. Stylized thread papers on ground of scattered origami papers. *Ōnishiki-ban*.

64. Stylized convolvulus vines on yellow ground; pattern is matched at top and bottom edges. *Ōnishiki-ban*.

65

66

65. Stylized portulaca sprigs in vertical pattern.
Ōnishiki-ban.

66. Highly stylized pattern of blossoms and leaves.
Ōnishiki-ban.

TAISHŌ-PERIOD CHIYOGAMI

大正時代の千代紙

60

*67. Rainy day: umbrellas and their shadows; designed by Yume-ji Takehisa. *Ōbōsho-ban*.

67

68. Leaves, blossoms, and tendrils in horizontal vine pattern; designed by Yumeji Takehisa. *Ōnishiki-ban*.

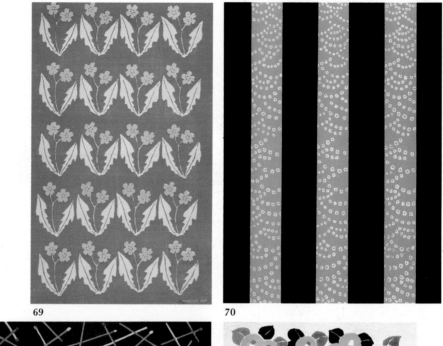

69

70

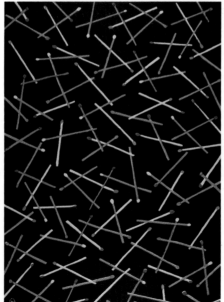

69. Primula sprigs on green ground; designed by Yumeji Takehisa. *Ōnishiki-ban*.

70. Dapple pattern alternating with black bands, reminiscent of a type of *obi* popular among young ladies of the Edo period; designed by Yumeji Takehisa. *Ōnishiki-ban*.

*71. Matches on black ground; designed by Yumeji Takehisa. *Ōbōsho-ban*.

72. Stylized pattern of camellia blossoms; designed by Yumeji Takehisa. *Ōnishiki-ban*.

71

72

Shōwa Period (1926–)

73

74

73. Fashionable furnishings for a Japanese art deco interior. *Ōnishiki-ban*.

74. Toys and playthings old and new, from *ane-sama* (upper left edge) to Mickey Mouse (upper right). *Ōnishiki-ban*.

75

75. Wooden *kokeshi*, lathe-turned dolls from northern Japan (detail). *Ōnishiki-ban*.

76. Assorted mechanical or moving toys, from old-fashioned tops to teddy bears. *Ōnishiki-ban*.

76

77. Scatter pattern of motifs relating to the fairy tale of Momotarō, the Peach Boy. *Ōnishiki-ban.*

78. Violets; from a series of designs for the twelve months by the popular illustrator Jun'ichi Nakahara; original prewar woodblock-printed edition. A recent revival of another pattern from the same series is shown in Plate 80. Onishiki-ban. Ca. 1940.

79. Ane-sama dolls: traditional paper figurines from Tottori Prefecture; designed and published by Shinpu Yamanouchi, founder of Go-Hachi Press. Onishiki-ban. Early 1940s.

80. Sunflowers; machine-printed replica of prewar design by Jun'ichi Nakahara; distributed by the magazine Ginga (Bunka Shuppan). Onishiki-ban. 1975.

81. Calico-style pattern of officers and ladies in Victorian costume; recent facsimile (hand-printed from recut blocks and issued by Go-Hachi Press) of 1935 original published by Hanga-so; designed by the noted print artist Sumio Kawakami.

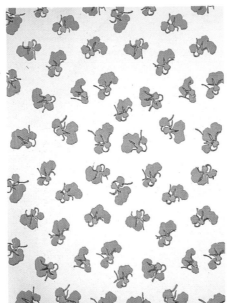

78

79

80

81

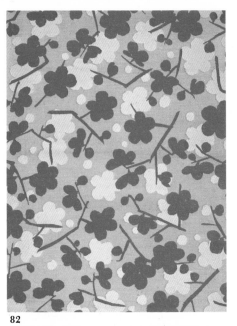

82

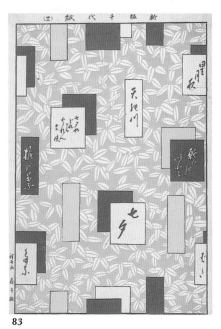

83

84

82. Red and white plum blossoms on pink ground; designed by Ryū-shi Kawabata for the Go-Hachi Press chiyogami steries; compare Plates 79 and 91. *Ōnishiki-ban. Ca.* 1942.

83. Poem-cards and bamboo decorations for the Star Festival on July 7; from a series designed by Shōko Suzuki for the publisher Senrei Sekioka. *Ōnishiki-ban.* 1930's.

84. Shells for the shell-matching game ornamented with plant motifs, geometric designs, and *Genji-kō* incense-game emblems; designed by Shōko Suzuki. *Ōbōsho-ban.*

85. Folded love-letters and pine needles on red ground. *Ōbōsho-ban*.

86. Portable lanterns bearing Kabuki actors' crests upon diagonal stripes reminiscent of the curtains for cherry-blossom-viewing parties; pattern refers to the Kabuki play *Tomo-yakko* ("The Man-at-Arms"). *Ōnishiki-ban*.

87. Schoolchildren's copybooks amid stylized blossoms on red and white checkered ground; design refers to the Kabuki play *Tenaraiko* ("The Schoolgirl"). *Ōnishiki-ban*.

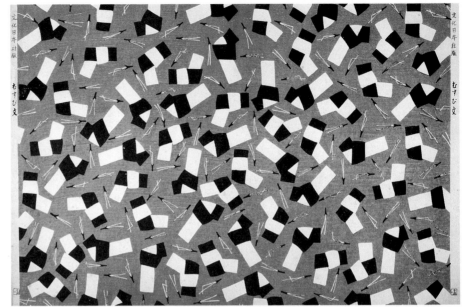

85

86

87

88

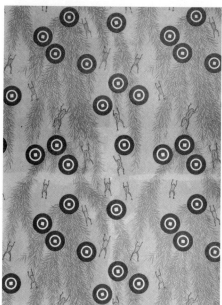

89

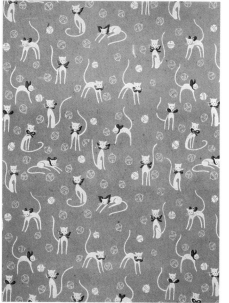

90

88. Kittens playing with silk balls amid stylized blossoms. *Ōbō-sho-ban*.

89. Early summer rains: willow boughs, frogs, and Japanese-style umbrellas viewed from above; pattern refers to the story of the calligrapher Ono no Tōfū; lithograph. *Ōnishiki-ban*. 1943.

90. Playful cats amid bells for cats' collars (detail); lithograph. *Ōnishiki-ban*.

91. Double-page spread from the magazine *Collection* (No. 64, June 1943), showing samples of woodblock chiyogami from the series issued by the publisher, Go-Hachi of Tokyo. The collotype plate at right reproduces an alphabet-based chiyogami pattern designed by Ryushi Kawabata; compare Plates 79 and 82.

91

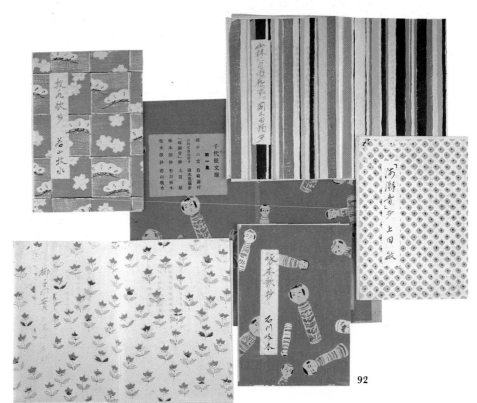

92. Chiyogami bunko ('The Chiyogami Library'), Series One (all published); poetry chapbooks with case and wrappers in chiyogami style; designed by Sachie Ogino and published by Fukujiro Yagi. 1947.

92

Modern Chiyogami

93

94

93. Stylized landscape repeated; recent reprint of 1935 original; designed by Sumio Kawakami. *Ōnishiki-ban.* Publisher: Go-Hachi (Tokyo).

94. Stylized landscape of Mt. Yoshino in spring. *Ōnishiki-ban.* Publisher: Ise-Tatsu (Tokyo).

95

96

97

95. Stylized water pattern with floating chrysanthemums and plum blossoms. *Ōnishiki-ban*. Publisher: Iwase (Tokyo).

96. Stylized water pattern with floating maple leaves. *Ōnishiki-ban*. Publisher: Sakurai-ya (Kyoto).

97. Autumn flowers and insects. Publisher: Miyamoto (Tokyo).

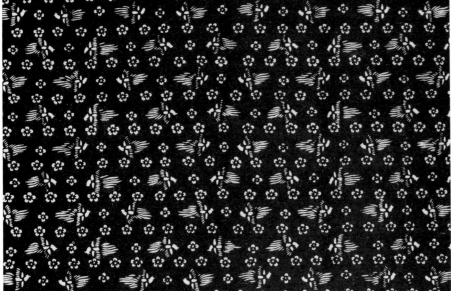

98. Maple leaves; designed by
Shōko Suzuki. *Ōnishiki-ban*. Publisher: Sekioka (Tokyo).

99. Pine, bamboo, and plum blossoms. *Ōbōsho-ban*. Publisher: Haibara (Tokyo).

100. Plum blossoms and flying
birds. *Ōnishiki-ban*. Publisher: Ten'-ichi-dō (Osaka).

101. Stylized wisteria blossoms on tripartite ground, with superimposed design of travelers' hats; design refers to the Kabuki play *Fuji-musume* ("The Wisteria Maiden"). *Ōnishiki-ban*. Publisher: Kobayashi (Tokyo).

102. Gion lanterns and stylized vertical fabric design reminiscent of a Kyoto dancing-girl's *obi*. Publisher: Sakurai-ya (Kyoto).

103. Patterns from Kabuki for *ane-sama* doll costumes. *Ōnishiki-ban*. Publisher: Sekioka (Tokyo).

104. Sixteen designs for Kabuki actors' make-up selected from *Ichikawa Jū-hachiban* ("Eighteen Classic Plays of the Ichikawa Family"). *Ōnishiki-ban*. Publisher: Igai Hanga-dō (Kyoto).

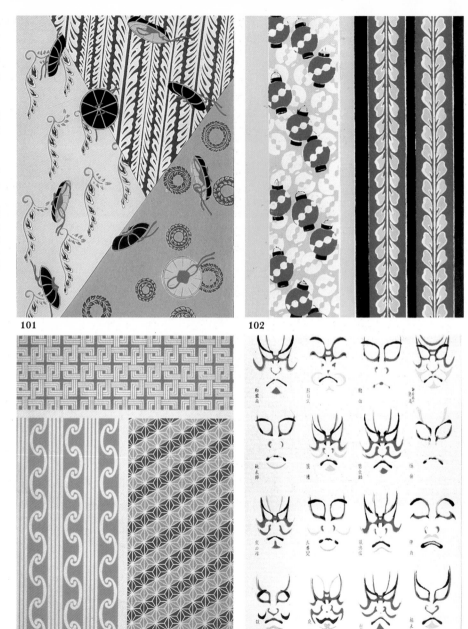

101

102

103

104

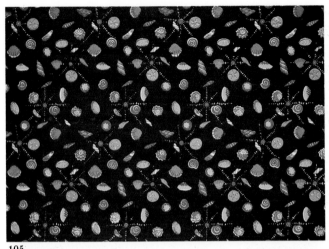

105

106

107

108

105. Shells in tie-dye pattern. *Ōbōsho-ban*. Publisher: Haibara (Tokyo).

106. Flower petals on textile-weave ground. *Ōnishiki-ban*. Publisher: Iwase (Tokyo).

107. Firework explosions against the evening sky; pattern refers to the annual July firework display held on the Sumida River in Tokyo. *Ōnishiki-ban*. Publisher: Miyamoto (Tokyo).

108. Fabric pattern of irregular stripes; design is available in assorted colors, of which four are shown here. *Ōnishiki-ban*. Publisher: Ten'ichi-dō (Osaka).

109

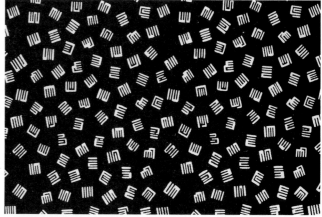

110

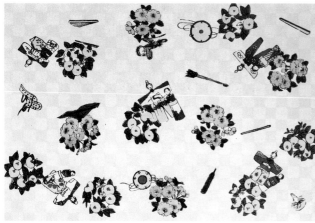

111

112

109. Modernistic geometric pattern; recent reprint from 1935 original; designed by Sumio Kawakami. *Ōnishiki-ban*. Publisher: Go-Hachi (Tokyo).

110. Scatter pattern of *Genji-kō* incense-game emblems. *Ōnishiki-ban*. Publisher: Igai Hanga-dō (Kyoto).

111. Dolls and other accessories for the Doll Festival on March 3. *Ōnishiki-ban*. Publisher: Ise-Tatsu (Tokyo).

112. Dance accessories on diagonal ground of cherry blossoms, red and white bell-ropes, and dancers' *obi* patterns; design refers to the Kabuki play *Dōjō-ji* ("Dōjō Temple"). *Ōnishiki-ban*. Publisher: Kobayashi (Tokyo).

千代紙の世界

アン・ヘリング

千代紙の世界

目次

〝千代紙〟という言葉は、国語教科書などに必ずしも登場するわけではないが、一般常識として知れ渡り、親しまれている。人々の年齢や生活体験、育った環境などの違いによって、この言葉から連想するイメージは人様々であろうが、また、そのような事実は千代紙の広がりと人々の千代紙に対する親しみの深さを示している。

　例えば、東京の多少とも余裕のある生活環境のもとで幼年期を過ごした年配の男性なら、大正の昔、ある雨の昼下がりに、色鮮やかな模様紙を切って、紙細工に夢中になっていた姉妹の姿を懐かしく思い浮かべるかも知れない。あるいは、地方出身の奥さんなら、幼い時に東京か京都から美しい千代紙をお土産に貰った思い出があるかも知れない。そしてまた、昭和生まれの女流作家や教育家、ジャーナリストの中には、終戦直後に、当時の女子学生が憧れた月刊誌「少女の友」に作文を投稿して、ご褒美に中原淳一の明るいモダンな千代紙を貰い、ますます作文に力を入れた方も、決して少なくはないはずである。

　最近の子供でも、文房具店へ行けば、呉服屋のショーウインドーにあるような美しい模様入りの折り紙を見付け、その帯に〝おりがみ〟でなく〝ちよがみ〟という題字が書かれているので、初めてその名前を覚えるというケースも珍しくない。このように、千代紙と

いう言葉は色々な人々の間に生き続け、その実情がよほど変わらないかぎり、死語になる心配はなさそうである。

千代紙とは

　千代紙とはそもそも何であろうか。実物の千代紙と深い縁のある人たちの間でも、その定義は完全に一致しているわけではないが、大雑把ながら以前からあるにはある。例えば包装紙との比較でいえば、それより丈夫でしなやか、しかも多少の腰がある紙であり、その上に、例の呉服屋の展示見本を連想させる豊かな色彩の、優美な模様が木版などで印刷されている。それがすなわち千代紙だと言えば、一般の人たちはおそらく納得するであろうが、特に千代紙に慣れ親しんでいる人は、昔ながらの木版手摺りのものこそ本物の千代紙である、と言い張るにちがいない。千代紙の歴史は勿論のこと、その質や美観から見れば、その主張にも確かに一理はあり、あながち否定はできない。

　と同時に、デパートや文具店、手芸専門店で盛んに売られている千代紙は、オフセット、シルク・スクリーン、型染めその他、木版手摺り以外の方法で刷られたものが主である。木版千代紙がいくら好きであるからと言って、その他の千代紙を無視することはやはり出来ないのが人情というもの。結局は、両方の千代紙を買い求める殆どの人々にとっては、木版か染め紙かオフセットか、などと言った印刷技法の問題よりも、模様や配色、そして何よりも先ず、手芸や人形作りなどの具体的な

使用目的に適っているかどうかという問題のほうが、はるかに大切なのである。たとえ木版でなくても、適当な模様があれば、千代紙としては充分役に立つ、という考え方である。このように、もっぱら模様本位に千代紙の品定めをする人々の意見にも一理はある。千代紙の歴史からみれば、むしろそのような考え方こそ本流であったと言えるであろう。

　約250年前と推定されている誕生の頃から今日に至るまで、千代紙はあくまでも消耗品であり、そのような応用芸術品として生き続けてきた。消費者の要求に合わせ、その好みに順応しながら、いわばしぶとく生きぬいてきたと言えよう。17世紀から18世紀にかけて、吹きぼかしや手彩色などの手仕事により、地味な模様に彩色されたと思われる千代紙は、素朴な単色の木版を経て、やがて江戸後期や明治の頃になると、華やかな多色摺り木版画に発展して全盛期を迎える。ここには印刷技術の発展、商品としての千代紙の売買、そしてまた、手芸などの材料に使う利用者の趣味の移り変わりが明白な形で反映している。このような適応性を千代紙のもう一つの特徴と見るならば、現在の機械印刷や手芸愛好家の要求にいとも機敏に適合する千代紙は、まさにその歴史的伝統を今日に生かし続けていることになる。

　しかしながら、千代紙はその適応性と美しさのみを取り得としていたならば、おそらく私たちの日常生活に、これほどしっかり根を下ろすことは出来なかったであろう。オフセット等による千代紙の売行きが良いとはいえ、

総て新しい技法に頼っているわけではない。宝暦・明和の頃から用いられた木版手摺りの千代紙は、少なくとも10ヵ所の版元や紙の専門店や画廊などで、今でも盛んに生産販売されている。錦絵の時代から今日に及ぶ木版印刷のジャンルは、千社札やご祝儀袋など、あまり多くはないが、まさに千代紙もその一つに数え入れることが出来るのである。つまり千代紙は、部分的には環境の変化に適応し変容しながらも、さらにまた、従来の大方の趣向を引き継いでいくという能力をも、同時に持ち合わせているわけである。

これは、木版という技法やその独特の味わいだけに限られる現象ではない。例えば模様に関して言えば、吉祥模様や花小紋、源氏香など、千代紙の初期に使われたもので今日の千代紙に欠かせない模様はいくつもある。この関連で面白いのは、色々な時代に生まれた新しい模様や形式をそのまま受け継ぎ、それらを共存させながら伝え続けるという千代紙の貪欲な生命力である。寛政以前からあった松竹梅や源氏香模様のものと並んで、幕末、明治、大正、昭和初期に至る各時代から受け継いだと思われる模様が、今でも盛んに刷られていて、様々な人々に買い求められている。購入した人の多くは、必ずしも江戸とか大正を問題にしているわけではあるまい。綺麗で、使用目的に合っているかどうか……結局は模様本位で勝負が決まるのである。昔も今も、この状況は変わらない。そして、それが変わらない限り、辞書の中の〝千代紙〟という単語も、そしてまた、商品としての木版千代紙も永遠に不滅である。

誕生から明治まで

模様本位で千代紙を選ぶ利用者と客本位で作る版元が、千代紙の実物や歴史について、わざわざ記録を残す必要を感じなかったとしても不思議ではない。特に近世の千代紙の場合、偶然に完全な姿で残されている実物も幾つかあるが、それ以外は手文庫などにたまたま残された切れ端を除くと、その記録は手紙や日記、出版社や紙問屋の広告などの、2次的文献に頼らざるをえないのである。

ところで、初期の千代紙はこれまで主に和紙一般の歴史という角度から、すでに故関義城氏らによって多少とも研究されてきた。最近は『千代紙集成』の著者森田康敬氏や『京のからかみと千代紙』の久米康生氏の努力のお陰で、18世紀の千代紙とその周辺のことがかなり明らかになりつつある。しかし皮肉にも、幕末や明治以降の千代紙の実態に関しては、新しい時代のことなのに、確かな情報があまり多く伝えられていない。懐古的な立場から消えていく千代紙をいとおしむ最近の傾向は、しかしながら、すでに大正期に現われていた。案外、そんな嘆き声をあげた人々の多くは、千代紙をあまりにも観念的に把えて、自分の身近な所で逞しく生き続けている千代紙の存在を、つい見落としてしまうことがあったのかも知れない。

幕末から明治、そして大正から戦中期にかけて、千代紙は江戸時代に引き続き、第2、第3の黄金時代を迎えたのではなかったか、

と推定させる資料がいくつかある。今日に残された、それぞれの時代から伝わる千代紙の実物は、まず何よりの証拠物件になろう。そしてまた、必ずしも確かな情報とは言えないまでも、そのような推定をある程度まで裏付け、または可能にするような2次的資料も、僅かながら存在している。ちなみに、幕末の英国大使ヘアリー・パークス公が江戸からロンドンへ送った和紙見本、あるいは欧米の博物館や美術館に現存している千代紙や模様紙、その他にも、明治・大正期に海外へ輸出された様々の和紙は、いずれ将来、近代の千代紙を知るための大切な手掛かりになるものと思われる。

しかし、それにしても、千代紙の歴史が比較的古いわりに、多少まとまった形で千代紙を話題にする書物は意外に少ないし、その上に、さほど古い昔からそれらが伝えられてきたわけでもない。千代紙を扱った最も古いと思われる文献は、筆者の知るかぎり、大正8年位まで遡れそうである。京都で発行された古樵亭山人の『古代千代紙』がそれである。図版はたっぷりと入ってはいるものの、序文も解説も全くなく、一種の"大人の絵本"と見てよかろう（その表紙になっている優雅な模様紙は、第26図に紹介されている）。鈴木三重吉の『千代紙』という単行本は、それより12年前の明治40年に出版されてはいるが、それはあくまでも小説集である。表題の「千代紙」も、内容に関わりがあるわけでもなく、象徴的な意味を担っているにすぎない。それにしても、三重吉が読者に通じるであろうと

いう自信をもって、千代紙のイメージを用いたこと自体、明治末期の社会と千代紙との関わりを暗示する資料の一つと言えるかもしれない。

ところで、その三重吉の初期の単行本の一つに、『千代紙』と同様の印象を私たちに与えるばかりか、それを一層具体的な姿で提示する短編集がある。明治45年に春陽堂から発行された『お三津さん』という本であるが、特にその装幀は千代紙の社会史を考えるうえで示唆に富むものである。表表紙から裏表紙へ一つの張り混ぜ式の絵が続いている。よく見ると、それらは幕末・明治の時代に流行ったおもちゃ絵の類い（両面合わせ人形、影絵、それに、あねさま衣装）と千代紙とを一つの模様に合わせたものと判る。『お三津さん』の装幀を担当した青年画家鏑木清方は、やがて20世紀の日本画を代表する芸術家として認められ、今日でも名高いが、歌川国芳の系統を受け継いでいるだけに、千代紙やこの紙を支えてきたかつての町人貴族たちの世界と、意外にも縁の深い画家であった。『お三津さん』の裏表紙を飾る千代紙模様は、その頃市販されていた千代紙を模写したものか、あるいは自ら考案したものなのか明らかではない。が、清楚な友禅風の模様で、明治後期の東京で実際に流行った半紙判の高級千代紙と非常によく似ている（英文解説第2図）。

大正デモクラシー前後

しゃれた装幀の『お三津さん』が世に出て暫くすると、三重吉や清方以外の文化人や趣

味人たちの間に、千代紙への関心が高まりつつある兆候がいくつも現われた。大正初期の頃、関岡扇太郎（初代扇令）、橋田素山、梅堂国政など、江戸文化に興味をもつ何人かの通人が、明治20年に亡くなった国芳の弟子、歌川芳藤の遺作を中心に、数回にわたって木版復刻シリーズを出版した。少年少女向けの、古い双六や絵草紙類の縮小版であったが、それらを畳紙に入れ、仲間の趣味人や希望者に配布したという。復刻の対象として考えられたのは、千代紙の親戚とはいえ別のジャンルの、いわゆる〝おもちゃ絵〟類が圧倒的に多かったが、それに混じって何種類かの千代紙もあった。芳藤の名入りの実物の千代紙があまり発見されていない今日、それらの縮小復刻版は実物を知るうえで、重要な手掛かりとなるのである（図版41）。

　大正末から昭和初期になると、今でも手広く活動を続けているいせ辰（当時は伊勢辰）の先代広瀬菊雄が復刻調の小型おもちゃ絵の発行と頒布会方式の販売に乗り出したが、おそらく、この温古木版印刷会発行の「芳藤手遊絵尽」のシリーズをかなり参考にしたのではないかと思われる。その当時、数々の版下絵を担当した鈴木祥湖という画家が、伊勢辰のために新案の千代紙を描いているが、その中には、現在でも売れている千代紙がかなりある。

　しかしそれより先、大正の中葉頃であったが、「大供」というおもちゃ類を趣味にする同人誌的な雑誌が創刊されて、千代紙はかなり広範な読者層の間で、あらためて注目を浴びるようになった。児童文学者であり、博文館編集部の大黒柱でもあった巌谷小波を中心とする「大供」の同人仲間は、現在も続けられている郷土玩具の収集や、日本古来の遊戯文化を見直す運動の先駆として、〝子供〟の上をいく〝大供〟たちであった。広瀬菊雄もその同人の一人として投稿もし、広告をも出して、この雑誌の表紙絵には伊勢辰版の千代紙が沢山使われた時もあった（英文解説第5図）。広瀬がその後、ますます千代紙に力を入れるようになり、自ら『千代紙百種　鶴』という総色摺りの千代紙図鑑を大正11年に出したのは、「大供」と何らかの関係があったのではないかと思われる。雑誌として「大供」はあまり長続きしなかったが、郷土玩具趣味に関してだけでなく、大正から昭和10年代にかけて高まっていく千代紙流行の引き金になったことは、間違いない。

　「大供」の同人仲間が、千代紙を懐古趣味の対象にしていた同じ大正期に、モダニズムを取り入れ、新しい千代紙作りを目指した人もいた。大正3年に、日本橋呉服町に港屋という小間物屋を開店した竹久夢二は、その商売のために数種類の千代紙を創作してハイカラなMINATOYA商標のローマ字を入れて売り出した。その総てが本来の千代紙の目的を達しているとは言えないが、夢二らしい特徴的なデザインがかなりある。その自由奔放な雰囲気は、それまでの千代紙にはあまり見られなかった斬新なもので、その後におけるモダン好みの千代紙のお手本になった（図版67―72）。

また、東京本郷にあった思成堂は、はたして港屋以前の創立かどうかはっきりしないが、アール・ヌーボーその他の20世紀の新流派の影響が、思成堂版千代紙の図柄に明白な形で現われている（図版55、60）。そして京都では、さくら井屋とピョンピョン堂から次々に登場した新柄の千代紙に、〝大正デモクラシー〟の時代色が様々な形で巧みに表現されている。そのモダニズムの系統は、やがて大阪の柳屋と東京の吾八に、部分的にせよ、受け継がれていくようになった。

石版千代紙が普及し、少女雑誌等に千代紙が登場したのも、大正の頃からではないかと思われる。「少女の友」の大正11年の新年号の付録には、「千代紙双六」が現われたが、これは一つの時代色を表わす出来事と言えるだろう（英文解説第3図）。

昭和の千代紙

昭和17年6月に、あねさま研究の権威稲垣武雄の〈愛玩会〉の協力を得て、江戸文化の民間研究家でもあった漫画家宮尾しげをが、「竹とんぼ叢書」の第1巻にあたる『昭和千代紙撰集・伊勢辰板之巻』を世に出した。戦時中にしてはかなり豪華な本で、題名にある通り、当時の伊勢辰の在庫千代紙31種類が実物見本入りで紹介され、広瀬辰五郎翁（菊雄）がかつて「星岡」などで発表した連載記事やその思い出話をもとに、宮尾しげをがまとめた「千代紙の話」も収録されている。この本から丁度1年後に、吾八発行の「これくしょん」（図版91）が千代紙特集の64号目で休刊を

余儀なくされ、千代紙の第3の発展期は終わりを告げる。

このような結果に至ったとはいえ、『お三津さん』の発行や夢二の港屋開店から、約30年間続いてきた趣味人や知識人たちの千代紙に対する情熱は、なぜか大正デモクラシーの敗退や満州事変以降にも冷めるどころか、ますます強まる傾向を見せてきた。漫画家の鋭い眼で、世間の風潮を観察してきた宮尾しげをは、さすがにこの流れに気付いていたようである。「昭和14年以来、久しく鳴りを鎮めていた千代紙が、急劇に意外な程に流行り出した。戦争と千代紙とは相当な関係があるのは研究に價する」というふうに、『昭和千代紙撰集』の後書きで述べている。結局のところ、時代が暗く不安になればなるほど、心ある人々は千代紙のような、無邪気で美しいものの中に、進んで心の安らぎを求めたのであろう。

千代紙の歴史に造詣の深い伊藤陸郎氏によれば、木版手摺りの良質の千代紙が最も数多く発行されたのは、1930年代前後であったそうである。これも、まさに宮尾しげをが指摘したように、〝戦争と千代紙〟の関係を裏付ける1例と言えよう。港屋の版木を宝物のように扱っていた大阪の柳屋、もみぢ屋、京都では大正デモクラシーの明るい面影を古都らしい形と結びあわせ、独特の千代紙を創作した鳥井さくら井屋とピョンピョン堂。東京では老舗の榛原や伊勢辰。そしてまた、昭和10年頃、鈴木祥湖の見事な新案千代紙シリーズを発表して、頒布会の案内状を最後の戯作者鴬亭金升に書かせた関岡扇令。うさぎ屋、三宅

松影堂その他、関東地方で戦中まで活躍していたと思われる版元の数々。戦争の前夜から今日まで無事に生き残った彼らの千代紙の殆どは、平和そのものである。俗悪なものも同時に売られたであろうが、昭和初期に市販されていた千代紙には、前述の竹久夢二や鈴木祥湖の他、川端龍子、川崎巨泉、前川千帆、川上澄生、中原淳一、それに宮尾しげを自身の筆によるものもあった。

龍子の新案や夢二の遺作、江戸時代ゆかりの源氏香、フランスのモダンなおもちゃやソ連の民芸品、古今東西からの画題を生き生きと、千代紙らしい新シリーズの中に取り入れた吾八が、「これくしょん」という洒落た月刊誌を創刊したのは、昭和12年であった。しかし、時代が時代だけに、この雑誌も昭和18年6月についに休刊の憂き目をみた。その編集者今村秀太郎氏は、最後の特集で新たに〝吾八の千代紙〟を実物の見本入りで紹介したが、そこには平和な世の中への熱い願いが、密かに込められていたのであろう。

それより4年後の昭和22年、平和になったとはいえ、灰色一色の世の中に少しでも明るさを取り戻そうと、八木福次郎氏の骨折りで、『千代紙文庫』という詩歌の豆本シリーズが発行されて広く話題を呼んだ（図版92）。同じ頃、明治からあった「少女の友」は内山基の後任、森田淳二郎の方針により、全国の少女たちに新しい希望の光を投げかけていた。戦時中、白い眼で見られていた中原淳一のデザインによる千代紙を、しばらくの間、投稿した読者あてに賞品として贈り続けたのは、この月刊誌であった。『千代紙文庫』を喜び迎え入れた文化人と、淳一千代紙に励まされた文学少女たちの幅広い支えがあって、千代紙は見事に蘇ったと言えよう。清方や夢二以来、平和の象徴とされてきた千代紙は、こうして戦後の、そして今日の世界への第一歩を踏み出したのである。

図版解説

＊印はいせ辰（広瀬辰五郎氏）蔵。他は総て著者の所蔵。

千代紙の寸法

大奉書判　約54×39cm

小奉書判　約47×33cm

大錦判　約39×27cm

2-3ページ　牡丹　大輪の牡丹を色々な角度から大胆に描いた模様。アニリン系の赤が使用されているので、明治初期の後摺りの可能性もあるが、輸入された顔料は幕末から使われていた。文久2年　白正堂版

6ページ＊　小さいお母さま　竹久夢二筆。夢二自らのデザインによる千代紙を部屋中に散らかした少女が、あねさま作りに無我夢中。雑誌『新家庭』より。大正6年。

7ページ＊　有平縞　赤白青の有平糖から名付けられた洒落た縞模様。『昭和千代紙撰集』（昭和17年）には、一番更紗写　伊勢辰案として紹介されている。

千代紙以前（江戸中期）

＊1.　内曇　天に藍、地に紫の雲形を漉き込んだもの。色紙、短冊などに用いた。小奉書判

＊2.　簾模様　本物の簾を版木代わりに用いて摺った地模様に、3色の暈し模様を加えたもの。簾だけでなく石その他手頃なものを使った例がある。小奉書判

＊3.　吹きぼかし　春の草花　霧吹器に絵の具を入れ息で紙の上に吹き飛ばす、又は、金網の上で絵の具をつけた刷毛をこすって施す模様を、吹き又は吹きぼかしと言う。赤と藍と緑の吹きぼかしに、肉筆や型紙で桜、蒲公英、蕨、菫など春の草花が描かれている。この類いの模様紙は、江戸中期・後期に京都で盛んに作られた。小奉書判

4.　吹きぼかし　松に鶴　前図の桜の花びら同様、鶴の姿に胡粉が用いられている。浜辺の感じを出すために、吹きぼかしが巧みに使われている。小奉書判

＊5.　墨流し　ヨーロッパの大理石模様の日本版とでも言うべきもの。中国より伝わったと思われる墨流しは、漉き模様と並んで最も歴史の古い模様紙の一つである。小奉書判

＊6.　墨流し（木版）　手作りの墨流し模様をそのまま木版で模倣したもの。小奉書判

江戸時代の千代紙

7.　菊　紙面の隅から隅までびっしり詰まった菊の花の数々。白菊の花びらが空摺りにより、立体的に表わされている。天保頃の作か。小奉書判

8.　牡丹　江戸中期・後期を通じて最も好まれた模様。極端に派手で大柄な模様が

千代紙に流行した。安政5年　小奉書判

9．牡丹　藍色の地色がわずか覗く程度で紙面一杯に派手な牡丹の花と蕾が描かれている。小奉書判

10．牡丹　紺色の潰し（地色）に7輪の極大の牡丹が、前図より写実的に表わされている。小奉書判

11．桜　紅の潰しに、浮くように描かれた白い花びらに緑がアクセントとして巧みに使われている。慶応2年　小奉書判

12．小桜　落ち着いた紅、鴬、茄子色による花小紋。控え目ではあるが、優雅で美しい江戸後期の代表的千代紙。小奉書判

13．鳳凰　大小の円形に抽象化された鳳凰模様。唐紙風の模様紙で、天地は模様が続く、いわゆる〝送り〟の技法が取り入れられている。小奉書判

14．松竹梅　前図と同様唐紙風の模様紙。抽象化された鶴亀松竹梅のおめでたい模様。天地左右が送りになっている。小奉書判

15．牡丹に飛鳥　黄と紅の牡丹の上に優雅に舞う、黄と茄子色の鳳凰。送りにはなっていないが、雰囲気や色彩から言って唐紙風の京都製千代紙と思われる。小奉書判

16．源氏香　江戸後期の典型的な細かい模様。テーマは「源氏香」と呼ばれる、香を使った遊戯に使われる記号。これは、組み香の基本となる5種の香を示すもので、5本の線の組み合わせによりできる52の形式を、始めの巻の「桐壺」と結びの「夢浮橋」の2帖を除く『源氏物語』の各帖の巻名に配したもの。源氏香の印が、京都の上流社会に現われたのは後水尾天皇の頃とされるが、その後本来の組み香の枠を出て、様々な分野に於いて抽象模様として使われるようになった。本図には更に葵の葉と源氏車が描かれ『源氏物語』ゆかりの雰囲気を高めている。安政4年　小奉書判

＊17．十二支　切り金を思わせる黄色の地模様に、十二支の動物たちと、亀、鈴等の縁起物が紙面一杯に散らされている。安政2年　小奉書判

＊18．縁起物尽くし　市川家の牡丹を施した凧、福助などの縁起物と藤、芙蓉など四季の花。安政5年　小奉書判

19．十二ヵ月　正月のかるた、2月の初午の狐面など、初春から暮までの年中行事の風物詩。幕末（後摺りか）　小奉書判

20．歌舞伎役者紋（残欠）八代目市川団十郎の瓢簞印など役者の紋の他、長唄、常磐津諸派の紋も見える。弘化・嘉永の頃

21．台所道具　おもちゃ絵と千代紙の中間的なもの。大型の紙を6枚に切って使うよう工夫されている。小奉書判

＊22．植木鉢尽くし　それぞれの植木鉢には歌舞伎役者の家紋がつけられている。小奉書判

23．抽象模様　唐紙風の暈し模様、赤と緑の2色の他に、白の地色も効果的に使われている。大奉書判

＊24．抽象模様　同じ唐紙風ではあるが、前

図より細かい。赤と銀の２色摺り。大奉
書判

＊25．抽象模様　観世水の一種で、紺と水色
の２色摺りに暈しが加えられている。大
奉書判

26．染め分け模様　藍と紅の対照と松皮菱
取りの大胆な線によって、二つの異質な
模様が見事に調和している。『古代千代
紙集』（大正８年）の表紙に使用された。
小奉書判

明治時代の千代紙

27．嵯峨菊　いかにも明治らしい、写実性
を巧みに取り入れた大柄な花模様。天地
が送りになっている。おもだかや版　大
錦判

28．菊　数種類の菊の花の間を蝶が舞い遊
ぶ。比較的細かい模様ながら、四方が送
りになっている。越米製（松野米次郎）
大錦判

29．「春秋」『美工図鑑』上巻（長谷川契
華　明治27年　京都発行）より。この本に
は後に千代紙の模様の参考資料になった
と思われる図が、かなり載っている。

＊30．花と紅葉　前図に基づくかどうか定か
ではないが、非常によく似た模様。大奉
書判

31．墨田川　『伊勢物語』の東下りに因ん
だ、友禅風の模様。牧金之助版　明治34
年　大錦判

＊32．扇面流し　観世水に浮かぶ四季折々の水
花模様の扇。四方送りになっている。秋

山武右衛門版　明治27年　大錦判

33．「金魚のあそび」　滑稽味のある金魚
と浮き草の散らし模様。今井敬太郎版
大錦判

34．羽衣　友禅模様風に抽象化された三保
の松原の松林と、浜辺に浮かぶように、天
女の羽衣が表わされている。尾関トヨ版
明治25年　大錦判

35．柏の葉に松葉　明治の人気画家川端玉
章が、明治末期に日本橋の榛原のために
描いた千代紙の一つ。大奉書判

36．四君子―梅竹蘭菊　蘭の葉を巧みに区
切りに利用した、斜め立涌の花模様。江
川版　大錦判

37．花青海波　春の水仙から晩秋の紅葉ま
で、四季の花々が青海波の形に色鮮やか
に描かれている。枠から飛び出した蘭が
アクセントとして一層効果的である。明
治の代表作。明治20年　大錦判

38．貝合せ　かるた遊びの一つの原型と思
われる貝合せ用の蛤形の枠に、花鳥模様
が描かれており、可憐で美しい。佐胺金
次郎版　大錦判

39．福助尽くし　凧上げ、魚つり、祭の行
列など、楽しい遊びに興じている福助。
見れば見る程面白くなる、人物中心の千
代紙。関西のものか。小奉書判

40．お福尽くし　よく遊び、よく働く明治
時代の女性の姿を、可愛らしいお福に見
立てた千代紙。前図の良き伴侶。小奉書判

41．格子縞に牡丹と鳳凰　歌川国芳の門人
の中でも、少年少女向けの出版美術に最

も貢献した一鵬斉芳藤の、現存する数少ない千代紙。玉川和助版　明治14年　大錦判

42．円形抽象模様　風車、雪輪、渦巻きなど、様々な丸い形を、鮮やかな赤紫の地色に散らした模様。大錦判

43．桜に蝶　明るい藤色の潰しに白い桜の花と模様化された蝶。明治の友禅風模様。大錦判

44．雪月花　雪、月、桜の花の大胆な輪郭の中に、それぞれ雪持笹、波千鳥の青海波、散る花びらが描かれている。大錦判

45．御所車　すやり雲と藤色の地に花霞を背景にして、源氏車と松の木を覗かせた友禅風の模様。明治35年　大錦判

46．菊桜　単に桜の花と言うより、桜と菊を重ねた花に、菊の葉が散らされ、色、形共、アクセント的役割りを果たしている。おもだか屋版　大錦判

＊47　朝顔棚　暈しによって立体感を出した、友禅風模様。大錦判

48．蕗　一応写実的に描かれた蕗ではあるが、葉の所々に紗綾形、観世水など、典型的な意匠模様の数々が施されている。大奉書判

49．鉄線　鉄線の花模様は、江戸後期・明治を通じて意外に人気があったようである。この千代紙の他にも鉄線模様が同じ版元から数多く出された。越米版（松野米次郎）　大錦判

50．潮に貝殻　抽象化された水を地模様に人手や蛤他様々な貝殻。白い紙を潰し代

わりにうまく生かした、明るく夏らしい涼しさを感じさせる千代紙。信国画　大錦判

51．折り鶴　三つの区分の内、下の二つは抽象化された鶴亀松竹梅で、一番上は浮き草と貝殻の模様。明治末期の典型的なスケールの大きい模様。明治35年　大錦判

52．弥次郎兵衛　青空と緑の芝生を連想させる薄い暈しの地色に、桜の花と弥次郎兵衛のおもちゃ。人形の弥次喜多の花見の見立てであろうか。明治の明るく洗練された友禅風の千代紙。大錦判

53．松に藤　昔から松に藤というのは、男女がそれぞれの特徴を生かして協力し合うたとえで、雛祭の調度にしばしば使われる。完全に抽象化されたこの植物模様は、節句用に作られたのであろうか。大奉書判

＊54．椿　色鮮やかな椿が画面一杯に表わされ、華やかな中にも品の良さを感じさせる千代紙。四方送りとなっている。大奉書判

55．紫陽花　染め物風の模様とは言え、配色にいくらかモダン好みの雰囲気が感じられる。版元は積極的にヨーロッパの影響を千代紙に取り入れようとした、東京本郷の思成堂。大錦判

56．葡萄　一見藤とも思われる模様は、葡萄と葉である。テーマも模様もあまり日本では見られないもので、ヨーロッパ・モダニズムの影響かと思われる。平野屋

版　大錦判

*57. 団扇散らし　明治かどうか断定しにく
いが、扇と同類のものとしてここで紹介
する。淡い色を効果的に使い、団扇の骨
に空摺りが用いられている。大錦判

*58. 扇面流し　豪華な染め模様を連想させ
る、派手な明治風千代紙。伝柴田是真
大奉書判

59. 扇面散らし　アニリン系の赤と紫なが
ら、きつい感じのない、いかにも明治ら
しい配色である。四方完全に送りになっ
ている。大錦判

60. 「春の調」正月の弾き初めの見立てであ
ろうか。三味線の糸と駒から成る洒落た
抽象模様。思成堂版　大錦判

大正時代の千代紙

61. 十二支　「娘道成寺」の黒繻子の帯模
様を思わせるデザイン。丸紋の中は十二
支の見立てになっている。大錦判

62. 宝尽くし　大正・昭和前期に流行した
と思われる黒の潰し。梅の花と亀甲形の
中に宝物が描かれている。大錦判

63. 糸巻き　いくらかアール・デコの影響
を受けた模様。画題は昔ながらの糸巻と
折り紙の散らし模様。四方送りになって
いる。図版63—66は総て「今古千代紙」可
久案　𝍀（花散里）板　大錦判

64. 朝顔　園芸用の朝顔の原型と思われる
形の花。花と蔓からなる、自然のままの
姿をやや抽象化した洒落たもの。四方送
りになっている。

65. 松葉牡丹　バウハウス式植物模様の日
本版とでも言えそうなモダンな花模様。
四方送りになっている。

66. 花市松　20世紀の始めに流行した、き
わめてモダンな配色の変わり市松模様。
抽象化された花と葉から成る。

*67. こうもり（洋傘）　伊勢辰から出され
た、竹久夢二の「どんたく千代紙」のシ
リーズのうちの１枚。雨の日を思わせる
斜めの傘一つ一つにその影がついている。
いかにも夢二らしい模様。大奉書判

68. 蔓草　赤と緑２色だけの素朴な配色な
がら、夢二の千代紙の中でも最も派手な
印象を与える模様の一つ。昔からある唐
草模様の夢二式バリエーション。柳屋版
大錦判

69. 桜草　大正３年から５年までの２年間
日本橋呉服町で、夢二と最初の妻たまき
が経営した港屋のためにデザインした千
代紙の一つ。後に版木が大阪の柳屋に移
り再発行されたので、柳屋名のものが多
く残っているが、これは珍しい港屋版
の初摺り。大錦判

70. 鹿の子　八百屋お七の帯を連想させる
江戸ゆかりの模様の、夢二による新解釈。
もとは港屋から出されたが、図版のもの
は柳屋版。よく似た模様が「どんたく千
代紙」に大奉書判で入れられている。大
錦判

*71. マッチの棒　やはり「どんたく千代紙」
のうちの１枚。思いもよらない画題とき
わめてモダンな配色には、夢二の機知が

72. 椿　68、70と同様柳屋版。黒、グレー、紅というやや地味な配色ではあるが、寒い季節に咲く花の落ち着いた美しさがよく出ている。大錦判

昭和前期の千代紙

73. 家具　「錦千代紙」という夢二などの影響を受けたシリーズのうちの1枚。夢二の千代紙同様、墨線を使わず自由奔放な線で描かれたモダンな家具調度類。1930年代に流行った電話や蓄音機、ピアノなどが時代を表わしている。大錦判

74. おもちゃ　前図と同様「錦千代紙」のシリーズ。昔ながらのあねさま、だるま、飛んだり跳ねたりなど懐かしいおもちゃと肩を並べているのは、ミッキーマウス、電気機関車、セルロイド人形など、当時としては最も新らしい舶来のおもちゃの数々。大錦判

75. こけし（部分）　大正の頃から流行したこけしが、他の郷土玩具と並んで、昭和初期、千代紙の画題として大いに取り入れられた。大錦判

76. 動くおもちゃ　ぜんまい仕掛けや車付きのものから、自由に動かせるぬいぐるみ、独楽、拳玉まで動くおもちゃの大行進。京都ピョンピョン堂の可愛らしい千代紙。大錦判

77. 桃太郎　張子のお面の犬、猿、雉子、鬼、五月人形の桃太郎、大判小判、宝物他桃太郎に因んだものの数々から成る可愛らしい散らし模様。大錦判

78. すみれの花　中原淳一は、昭和15年頃から千代紙にも筆を染めた。写真のものは、初版の木版手摺り千代紙。図版80は、姉妹品の複製である。大錦判。

79. 鳥取あねさまのつなぎ模様　発行元吾八の当時の社長・山内神斧自らの図案。吾八は、昭和初期以来の愛書家たちの溜まり場として有名。大錦判。

*80. ひまわり　終戦直後でも、中原淳一の戦前の千代紙は、一時期『少女の友』の賞品として使われた。印刷による数種の複製品はまた、昭和50年に雑誌『銀花』（文化出版局）から配布されることもあった。大錦判。

81. 士官と貴婦人　昭和10年頃、川上澄生が「ろまんちっく千代紙」を銀座の版画荘から出した。ヴィクトリア王朝風の男女は、澄生が少年期を過ごした明治後期の横浜の思い出に基づくものか。写真のものは最近の復刻。吾八版　大錦判

82. うめ　伝統的な紅白梅の模様ではあるが、画風は正にモダンそのもので夢二を連想させるものがある。20世紀日本の出版美術に新風を吹き込んだ、川端龍子のデザイン。吾八版　大錦判

83. 七夕　薄緑色の笹の葉の地模様に色紙、短冊の数々。天の川、星月夜からわかるように七夕祭を表わす洒落た模様。鈴木祥湖が関岡扇令のためにデザインしたもの。関岡版　大錦判

84. 貝合せ　墨版の代わりに藤色を使った

変わり源氏貝合せ模様。鈴木祥湖画　関岡版　大奉書判

85. 結び文　柔らかな赤地に紺と白の松葉と恋文。両端に題名、版元名、画家名が入っているのは、二つに切って大錦判として売ったものか。文化日本社版　大奉書判

86. 供奴　益川版の「舞踊千代紙」シリーズのうちの1枚。一人の役者が泣き上戸と笑い上戸を演じる、ユーモアあふれる歌舞伎の所作事に因んだ模様。大錦判

87. 手習子　同じく「舞踊千代紙」より。市松に手習草紙と椿、梅などの模様。女形の所作事の見立て。大錦判

88. 子猫と手鞠　鞠と戯れるいたずら子猫たち。千代紙にはあまり多くない猫模様の一つ。地色は赤、紫など色違いで出された。うさぎ屋版　大奉書判

89. 梅雨と子供　「千代紙子供の十二月」というシリーズのうちの1枚。戦時中、京都でこんな楽しい石版による千代紙が出された。小野道風と蛙の話の見立て。昭和18年　国民航空教材株式会社版　大錦判

90. 猫と鈴(部分)　足も尻尾も長いお洒落な猫と鈴の散らし模様。昭和前期の石版千代紙。

91. 「これくしょん」　吾八発行の雑誌「これくしょん」64　千代紙特集号に掲載された千代紙。昭和18年

92. 『千代紙文庫』　灰色一色の戦後の世の中に小さな明りを灯した豆本シリーズ、『千代紙文庫』第1集。表紙はそれぞれ異なった千代紙模様。昭和22年　荻野幸枝装幀　八木福次郎発行

現代の千代紙　　　(榛原版以外総て大錦判)

93. 山並　川上澄生「ろまんちっく千代紙」のうちの1枚。最近再発行されたもの。吾八（東京）

94. 吉野山　満開の桜が春の吉野山を思わせる優雅な千代紙。いせ辰（東京）

95. 観世水に花　濃紺の水に鮮やかな梅と菊の友禅風の模様。岩瀬（東京）

96. 観世水に紅葉　明るい紺地の水に流れる紅葉。葉脈は銀で摺られている。さくら井屋（京都）

97. 秋草に鈴虫　桔梗、女郎花、撫子など秋の七草の陰に鈴虫が鳴く。宮本（東京）

98. 紅葉　昔ながらの紅葉の散らし模様。鈴木祥湖画　関岡（東京）

99. 松竹梅　明るい藍色地に白抜きで細かく表わされた松竹梅。地味ではあるが応用範囲の広い千代紙。榛原（東京）　大奉書判

100. 花鳥　白抜きの花と鳥の散らし模様。地色は色違いで数種類出されている。猪飼（京都）

101. 藤娘　「舞踊千代紙」シリーズの再発行。日本舞踊や歌舞伎の藤娘に因んだ模様。小林（東京）

102. 提灯に帯　京都の都踊を連想させる祇園提灯と舞子の帯模様を取り入れた千代紙。さくら井屋（京都）

103.かぶき 「新版意匠千代紙」シリーズの一つ。あねさまの着物に利用される。美秀画 関岡（東京）

104.隈取り 助六、矢の根、暫など市川十八番の中からの代表的隈取り。猪飼（京都）

105.貝殻 紺地に様々な貝殻模様。榛原（東京） 大奉書判

106.花びら 地の、布目を使って出した模様は、江戸中期の模様紙（図版2）を思わせる。岩瀬（東京）

107.花火 隅田川の川開きの花火か。グレーの地色は夕暮を表わしている。宮本（東京）

108.縞 あねさま作りに欠かせない、各色の縞模様。天一堂（大阪）

109.幾何学模様 川上澄生のシックな黒とグレーの2色摺りの模様。吾八（東京）

110.源氏香 千代紙の最も古い模様の一つと思われる源氏香は、現在も相変わらず使われている。色違いで何色か出されている。猪飼（京都）

111.雛祭 淡いピンクと白の市松の地に、折り雛に代表される3月の節句に因んだものが散らされている。いせ辰（東京）

112.道成寺 「舞踊千代紙」シリーズの再発行。白拍子花子の帯や烏帽子などの組み合わせは歌舞伎の道成寺の見立てである。小林（東京）

序説中のモノクロ挿絵

1．渋川版の『はちかつぎ』の表紙（部分）。金銀の折り鶴模様。亨保頃、大阪。

2．鈴木三重吉著『お光さん』。千代紙模様の装丁：鏑木清方。明治45年、東京。

3．『少女千代紙双六』。明石精一画。「少女の友」第15巻1号付録。実業之日本社発行。大正11年、東京。

4．生活の中の千代紙。終戦直後の女学生が教科書のカバーに使った「クルミちゃん」模様の千代紙（ぴょんぴょん堂版）。

5．巌谷小波の玩具趣味雑誌「大供」。表紙の千代紙は、伊勢辰版。大正期。

6．「少女界」第4巻10号の表紙絵：あねさま。金港堂発行。明治35年、東京。

7．戯曲『義経千本桜』に由来する千代紙模様。明治20年代頃、東京。今井版。

8．生活の中の千代紙。明治後期の手作り十六武蔵。材料は、江戸期のの千代紙。

9．生活の中の千代紙。仮名垣魯文『魯文珍報』仮製本された合本。表紙は、源氏香模様の千代紙。明治23年頃、東京。

10．横山隆一氏の「フクちゃん」を（無許可？で）取り入れた石版千代紙。図版89の姉妹品。昭和18年、京都。

11．上方絵本『絵本龍宮遊』の表紙。行成好みの模様紙。18世紀後半、京阪。

12．18世紀の欧州でも、模様紙は、児童書の装丁用に流行した。『黄金の玉手箱』の見返し。1753年、ドイツのハレ市。

13．千代紙の宣伝広告。嘉永5年、江戸。

終わりに

　この本の完成は、じつに数多くの方々から数多くのお力添えを得て可能となった。それらの方々を漏れなく列挙して感謝の意を表わすことは、限られた紙面では不可能であるが、何はともあれ、その昔、留学生であった私を"千代紙の世界"に導き入れて下さった井垣ツヤ氏と田中千枝子氏、田中氏の恩師の故武藤喜邦・テウご夫妻とその一門の方々に、まず感謝の言葉を捧げたい。

　さらにまた、玩具文化史を手解きして下さった斎藤良輔氏、いつも良き相談相手になって下さった千代紙の第一人者伊藤陸郎氏、絶えず筆者を励まして下さった牧野玩太郎氏、〈竹とんぼの会〉、〈郷土玩具友の会〉、〈日本児童文学学会〉、〈武井武雄親類の会〉の会員の方々。古くから千代紙の調査に力を貸して下さった佐藤ひさし氏、宮本鎌一氏、遠藤寛子氏、村尾泰氏、吾八の今村秀太郎氏、稲城市の岩村よね氏、大阪の尾上政太郎氏。色々お骨折りを賜った岩瀬孝一氏と紙の博物館、それに森田康敬氏、二代目関岡扇令氏とみどり夫人。こうした数え切れぬ人たちのご好意には、まことに感謝の言葉もない。

　すでに故人となられたが、仁木悦子、南部宣国、瀬田貞二、鳥居徳三郎、山田徳兵衛、高根宏浩、夏目正三、御荘金吾、尾上多賀之丞、平塚武二それに稲垣武雄の各氏にも、この本をどんなにご覧に入れたかったことか。

　最後に、本書に序文を寄せられ、その上、貴重なご教示をいただき、多数の資料を提供して下さった4代目広瀬辰五郎氏、そして、講談社インターナショナル編集部の早川恵子氏に、改めて厚くお礼申し上げたい。

　尚、この本を全国の古書業界の皆様、そして本年めでたく米寿をお迎えになる菰池佐一郎氏に捧げたい。

　　1987丁卯年1月25日・初天神

　　　　　　　　　　　　アン・ヘリング

94

主要参考文献
Selected Bibliography

古樵亭山人『古代千代紙集』京都　松吉宇三郎
大正 8 年
〈Koshōtei-Sanjin. *Kodai chiyogami-shū.* Kyoto:
Usaburō Matsuyoshi, 1919.〉

広瀬辰五郎（3代）『千代紙百種　鶴』
東京　伊勢辰商店　大正11年
〈Hirose, Tatsugorō. *Chiyogami hyakushu-tsuru.*
Tokyo: Ise-Tatsu, 1922.〉

『千代紙色紙』京都　芸艸堂　昭和11年
〈*Chiyogami irogami.* Tokyo: Unsō-dō, 1936.〉

宮尾しげを　『昭和千代紙撰集』　東京　愛玩会
昭和17年
〈Miyao, Shigeo. *Showa chiyogami senshu.* Tokyo:
Aigan-kai, 1942.〉

『和紙研究』11号　京都　和紙研究会　昭和18年
〈*Washi kenkyū,* no. 11. Kyoto: Washi Kenkyū-kai,
1943.〉

『これくしょん』64号　東京　吾八　昭和18年
〈*Korekushon* (Collection), no. 64. Tokyo: Go-Hachi,
1943.〉

斎藤良輔『日本人形玩具辞典』東京　東京堂出版
昭和43年
〈Saitō, Ryōsuke. *Nihon ningyō gangu jiten.*
Tokyo: Tokyodō Shuppan, 1968.〉

広瀬辰五郎（4代）『江戸千代紙』東京　丸ノ内出版
昭和46年
〈Hirose, Tatsugorō. *Edo chiyogami.* Tokyo:
Marunouchi Shuppan, 1971.〉

『手漉和紙』　東京　毎日新聞社　昭和50年
〈*Tesuki washi.* Tokyo: Mainichi Shinbunsha, 1975.〉

広瀬辰五郎　『江戸千代紙いせ辰三代』
東京　徳間書店　昭和52年
〈Hirose, Tatsugorō. *Edo chiyogami Ise-Tatsu
sandai.* Tokyo: Tokuma Shoten, 1977.〉

『新撰紙鑑』（復刻版）　東京　紙の博物館　昭和52年
〈*Shinsen shikan* (facsimile edition). Tokyo: Paper
Museum, 1977.〉

『千代紙文様』　京都　京都書院　昭和54年
〈*Chiyogami monyō.* Kyoto: Kyoto Shoin, 1979.〉

森田康敬　『千代紙集成』
京都　ふたば書房　昭和57年
〈Morita, Yasutaka. *Chiyogami shūsei.* Kyoto:
Futaba Shobō, 1982.〉

久米康生『京のからかみと千代紙』
東京　雄松堂出版　昭和61年
〈Kume, Yasuo. *Kyo no karakami to chiyogami.*
Tokyo: Yūshōdō Shuppan, 1986.〉

木版手摺千代紙制作・販売店
Present-day publishers of
woodblock-printed chiyogami

いせ辰　〒110　東京都台東区谷中2-18-9　03-3823-1453
Ise-Tatsu:18-9, Yanaka2-chome, Taito-ku, Tokyo 110

岩瀬孝市　〒123　東京都足立区梅田6-21-15-106
03-3840-7843
Kōichi Iwase: 21-15-106, Umeda 6-chome, Adachi-ku,
Tokyo 123

吾八書房（ギャラリー吾八の後継者）
〒101　東京都千代田区神田神保町1-6　樋谷ビル4F
03-3292-0058
Go-Hachi: Kanda-Jinbocho 1-6, Chiyoda-ku, Tokyo 101

関岡扇令　〒116　東京都荒川区西日暮里3-11-8
03-3821-1892
Senrei Sekioka: 11-8, Nishi-Nippori 3-chome,
Arakawa-ku, Tokyo 116

榛原　〒103　東京都中央区日本橋2-7-6　03-3272-3801
Haibara: 7-6, Nihonbashi 2-chome, Chuo-ku, Tokyo 101

ゆしまの小林　〒113　東京都文京区湯島1-7-14（おりがみ会館）
03-3811-4025
Yushima no Kobayashi: 7-14, Yushima 1-chome,
Bunkyo-ku, Tokyo 113

猪飼版画堂　〒600　京都市下京区綾小路堺町角
075-351-7309
Igai-hangadō: Sakaimachi-kado, Ayanokoji, Shimogyo-
ku, Kyoto 600

京都ピョンピョン堂　〒606　京都市左京区下鴨西半木町37
075-711-0177
Kyoto Pyonpyon-dō: Nishihangi-cho 37, Shimogamo,
Sakyo-ku, Kyoto 606

さくら井屋　〒604　京都市中京区三条新京極角
075-221-4652
Sakurai-ya: Shinkyogoku-kado, Sanjo, Nakagyo-ku,
Kyoto 604

天一堂　〒537　大阪市東成区中道4-7-14
06-974-7400
Ten'ichi-dō: 7-14, Nakamichi 4-chome, Higashinari-ku,
Osaka 537

　尚、上記以外の木版手摺千代紙の制作者をご存知の
方は是非お知らせください。その他古い千代紙や版木
をお持ちの方、千代紙の懐かしい思い出のある方から
も、ご一報をお待ちしております。（著者）